MORE OF
THE MAGIC TOUCH

8 Successful Massage Therapists share "out of the box" business and marketing secrets

MEAGAN HOLUB L.M.T.

Olive Vine Press
Seattle, Washington

Published by Olive Vine Press for e MASSAGE, LLC

117 E. Louisa St. #449, Seattle WA 98102
Cover and book design by Andy Graef, Seattle, Washington
Edited by Nick Jenkins, Seattle, Washington

ISBN: 978-0-9823655-1-9

What good is money without sharing it?

A percentage of proceeds from the Magic Touch
will be donated to the following non-profit organizations:

www.kidsdonations.org
www.childhaven.org
www.freeartsnyc.org

Dedicated to grandma June.
Without you
I would never have loved myself
enough to follow my dreams.

~Meagan

CONTENTS

Leading a fascinating career from leaving a career as a professional dancer to regain his health he soon built the first chair massage business in Canada, sold it for half a million and continues to contribute to the Massage Therapy profession through Massage Therapy Radio, and the largest online Massage conference in the world. Eric not only provides solid reasons for not taking your role so seriously that you miss valuable opportunities for growth in business, but provides an in depth look at what strategies work and what falls flat in marketing a massage therapy business. As is apparent by his resume, we can all benefit by listening.

Laura is respected writer on the business and politics of Massage Therapy in both publications and journals, known for her no-apologies tone. She describes her climb from a first year salary of $16,000 to over $300,000 the fifth year in her Massage Therapy business and shares her unique approach to marketing which allowed her to reach the impressive goal of attracting over 365 new customers during a recession, a time which county had the second highest unemployment rate out of the 100 counties in North Carolina and the 13th worst in the nation. Every entrepreneur can benefit from the sensible low cost and no- cost marketing revealed.

Meagan, author and celebrity massage therapist spent the first seven years of her career figuring out how to develop necessary boundaries and business practices that would get her out of the "broke and burned out" cycle. After writing The Magic Touch, she was able to observe her somewhat counter-culture business advice held true during the very economic recession she had predicted three years before the fall. Now she shares inexpensive marketing strategies specifically for harsh economic times with the belief that businesses developed on old-fashioned standards of quality and value sprinkled with "out of the box" marketing strategies, will be recession- proof. Meagan reminds us that "what comes up must come down" and offers ways for you to enjoy the ride by thriving in any economic climate.

"Opportunity is a bird that never perches."

- Claude McDonald

1

ERIC BROWN

Eric gets his first massage...

Growing up in a small town in northern Canada, massage was something that never entered my consciousness at all. I didn't get massage from my siblings or my parents and I didn't give massages. The only memory I have of massage growing up was in a hospital. At about eight years of age I developed Idiopathic Perpera. It's a platelet disorder that caused me to bleed spontaneously under my skin. I was hospitalized for quite a number of weeks and backrubs were one of the daily hospital rituals. A nurse would come in, I'd take off my pajama top and lie face down on my bed and she'd do a quick rub down. I'm not sure if I liked it or not, but it was a strong memory from my hospital stay.

Massage certainly never entered my mind as a career choice at any point growing up. I decided to study business at university. I thought it would be good to have an accounting designation and that's where I focused my education. However, I was really an artist at heart and after taking part in a high school musical, I decided that I loved to dance. So I signed myself up for ballet classes. Remember, I was living is a small town in northern Canada. But surprisingly most people in my life were relatively supportive and I continued my dance training until I left for university.

That year was the first and last of my adventures in accounting. I discovered that you had to have an accountant's personality to do accounting. I didn't have one. I had to look elsewhere for career fulfillment.

In a moment of insanity, I decided I was going to be a professional dancer. So I began intense training in classical ballet. Through my professional training as a dancer, I suffered physically. I was pretty much in pain constantly as I pushed my flexibility and strength to the limits every single day of training.

Some of the dancers would get massage occasionally and they loved it. So I had to give it a try. My first experience was in this young woman's living room with a shrine set up over the fireplace.

She was a student massage therapist recommended by my chiropractor. That was my first whole body massage. I haven't to admit I felt extremely uncomfortable. I had never had anyone touch me all over like that before. I kind of liked it. It seemed like a strange and unusual experience but, overall, it was a good first taste of massage. After that, I went relatively regularly to a local massage school that offered discount student massages. On those rare occasions when I had a little extra money in my pocket I'd go see a "professional".

I had a short, but amazing career as a dancer. I even got to perform with the National Ballet of Canada. Why did I leave dance? Although I was working regularly, the pay was poor and I knew my career would be short. Working at the level and at the intensity I did, I simply hurt all the time. So in a somewhat difficult decision, I hung up my ballet shoes at the end of a run of performances and never did ballet again.

Becoming a massage therapist...

What could I possibly do after a career in dance? I liked getting massage as a dancer, so I considered getting some training.

The Sutherland-Chan School, one of the three available in Toronto, offered their 2,200 hour program in a compressed, intensive 18-month format, so I wouldn't have to spend years in school.

At that time I didn't see massage as being my final career, but at least I would have a skill to use to support me financially as I continued training in some other profession. I enrolled in January 1988. From the first day on, I was completely hooked on this incredible industry.

In my first year of training there were two things that struck me as remarkable. Both had an indelible influence on where I am today as a massage therapist.

The first is just how new, undeveloped and raw this industry was. For those therapists just coming into the field, it's hard to fathom how far the massage industry has come in just 20 years. We were still living in the massage prehistoric times in 1988 as I started my massage program. Several years previous in the USA, the AMTA had just dropped the titles of "masseur" and "masseuse" (which were still in use in our legislation at the time) in favor of "massage therapist".

There were no massage textbooks. None. Zero. Zilch. The only book specifically for massage therapists was a small massage guide that was written in the 50s by Frances Tappan. To that point there were only a handful of research studies done on massage, most from the 30s and 40s. Instructors had absolutely no information on which they could base what they were telling us was true about massage.

When I graduated, there were only about 800 therapists in the entire province of Ontario, Canada's most densely-populated province. And as I looked at my new registration number after being licensed and did some napkin math, it was clear that there had been on average no more than 40 new therapists coming into the field each year in Ontario over the previous five decades.

This was an industry in its infancy (and still is in many respects) and that meant a great number of opportunities in all aspects of the industry. This was a profession that was not entrenched and that could be shaped.

The second thing that struck me is that massage seemed to me to be a service that would never be mainstream. I was a dancer so I didn't have any real issues with being naked. We often had co-ed change rooms and we were touching each other in ways that were intimate all the time as dancers. It's just the nature of the job.

But even with my openness, I kept thinking that there was no way North Americans as a whole would feel comfortable with this sensuous (not sexual) type of service.

I loved my massage training. I particularly liked getting massage regularly. It was as if I craved being touched. I really couldn't get enough.

And I loved massaging people. The instant sense of gratification for having made someone feel better was addictive. I knew when someone hopped off my table at the end of a session they were going to feel better than when they came in, whether or not I fixed their injury.

I could also see the need that people had to be touched. I didn't appreciate this as much at first, but I soon came to realize that people weren't really coming in for massage because of their pain issues or injuries. We are trained as paramedical professionals here in Canada with standards similar to other healthcare practitioners, so customers could just as easily have seen a physical therapist or chiropractor whose fees were covered or subsidized under our socialized medical system at the time. It was evident that they came for massage mostly because they just wanted to be touched.

The idea of providing structured touch to a touch-starved society was an important one for me. It's where I saw the true power of massage. It is the one thing that truly defines massage as being unique from the other health disciplines. This became the major theme in my life and career as a massage therapist and continues to be the driving force behind everything I do.

Starting up...

After graduation, I was a man on fire. I really wanted to move this young industry forward. In my mind, massage had to overcome its association with the sex trade and become more acceptable to the medical profession and the mainstream public.

One of the first projects I worked on was a fundamentals massage textbook with Mosby, a large American publisher. I and a number of co-authors wanted to establish a scientific basis for the work we did in the classroom and under contract with Mosby began to write the first research-based textbook. This consumed about four years of my life as I wandered through the halls of medical libraries in hospitals and universities compiling and devouring pretty much every research paper that had been written on massage in the past century. I had banker boxes filled with studies and tried to make sense of them all, looking for the threads of connection. In the process I became THE expert in massage therapy and the scientific mechanisms for its effects. Unfortunately, I never got to share that knowledge in printed form.

As we were finishing the book, it became clear to the Mosby editors that this would not sell in the USA. They needed a book that showed students how to cover a client with a sheet properly, not one that outlined the mechanisms of cancer metastasis and the role massage played in that. So they commissioned Sandy Fritz to write a basic textbook. Although my book was not published, she had access to our materials and at least bits of what we researched were summarized in her book.

The knowledge I gained in the process made me a real content expert and I began teaching at local colleges almost immediately after graduation. I didn't teach just a little, I taught a heavy course load. I figured I taught well over 1,000 therapists in 2,200 programs in my first six years as an educator. Much of my job was developing curriculum and since oftentimes there was not really any solid curriculum in place, I became a real expert at structuring training processes.

Of course, immediately upon graduation, I started my own private practice. I rented a room from a chiropractor I used to see as a dancer. He treated many of the dancers from the National Ballet and he suggested I come and work with him after graduation. So I targeted dancers as a market. It was a market I knew well. My professional practice filled very quickly. Within several months I had a full schedule of clients.

I was not going to make a living massaging dancers, however, because dancers are not known for being particularly well-off financially. So I had to expand my reach. I knew it was important to target a particular group of people if you wanted to be successful: "Finding a niche will make you rich." This is an important lesson for any new therapist to learn quickly. Especially as the market becomes more saturated with massage therapists, you cannot afford to be a generalist.

This chiropractor's office was located in the Village in Toronto, essentially the gay area of the city. In the early 90s, HIV infection was a big issue in that community. They were just starting to understand the mechanisms of transmission, but people who had been infected years earlier were starting to become symptomatic and there was no effective way of managing the disease. So there were a lot of people developing AIDS and what they needed essentially was palliative care.

HIV-infected individuals were people who needed massage. They didn't necessarily have physical issues that I could address, but they needed to be touched. I had no problem doing that.

My approach to this market was multifaceted. You'd be wise to take a similar kind of approach when targeting a group of your own. With this kind of approach you become so tied into a community of people that your name starts showing up everywhere. It's a little bit of "shock and awe" strategy: identify a small target, hit from every direction and do it fast. Here are some of the tactics I used:

- I contacted every social service agency that dealt with HIV patients and offered to go in at least once to massage the staff for free. These were key influencers.

- Through networking and direct contact, I let doctors and other health professionals in the area know that I specialized in HIV patients.

- When I treated an HIV patient, I would get their permission to write their doctor a note to let them know I was treating them and to advise me if there were any factors I needed to take into consideration specifically when treating this individual. This quickly helped me become recognized among doctors as the massage therapist to refer their HIV patients to.

- I wrote articles for newsletters of support groups.

- I offered to do free introductory workshops for the members of these support groups if the group was willing to support and host them.

- In all my community advertising I made it clear that I specialized in HIV patients.
- I did locums for the massage therapist at the local hospice.
- And of course, I asked for referrals.

The strategy worked. Within a short time I became the person to see if you had HIV. I was the expert. At one point, more than half the clients in my busy practice were HIV-positive.

This led to other opportunities. My expertise in palliative care and working with complicated conditions even got me a job working with cancer patients at a medical center.

But working with the dying took its toll on me emotionally. I was able to maintain a certain level of professional distance, but I had clients dying pretty much every week. So I decided to scale down that aspect of my practice.

At the same time, I moved from the chiropractor's office where I had been working and set up a home practice. It made sense because I was teaching so much and focusing on my textbook and although I had a very full schedule of massage clients, I just wasn't using the space full-time and couldn't justify spending the amount of money I was spending.

I made the mistake that I think a lot of therapists make. I felt that the chiropractor was getting too much out of the arrangement. It seemed unfair to me. I was successful and paying him both a flat fee and a percentage of my sales. But what I didn't realize is that it really was an investment in my continued success and simply the cost of doing business.

I saw it as an expense, but it really was an investment. I wasn't just paying for a little space of real estate; I was paying for walk-in traffic, direct referrals from the chiropractor, visibility to chiropractic patients and referrals from them, a receptionist and collegial support from the chiropractor and others who worked at the clinic.

The combination of changing locations, losing my base of chiropractic patients, dropping my marketing to HIV patients, along with increasing competition in my community caused my private practice to suffer terribly. I floated aimlessly in my approach to marketing my practice. By 1994, just five years after graduating, my practice bottomed out. I remember the day when I literally cried with frustration. Pretty much everything that I had built until then was now gone.

But it's moments of desperation that are often moments of new beginnings and that's exactly what happened. I realized if I continued doing what I was doing I would get absolutely nowhere. So at that moment I made the commitment to change my practice and my life.

If I were to give the two keys to being successful, I would have to say making an unflinching commitment to a defined goal and taking massive action to achieve that goal.

And that's what I did. Before the end of the year I had two multi-therapist clinics and they were both off to a strong start. There was no particular secret to ramping them up. I just did the things that I knew worked and I did them consistently and in a big way. I chose a couple of key marketing strategies and executed them fully. I'll share some of those in a moment.

Discovering chair massage...

The other discovery I made that year was chair massage. David Palmer came to Toronto to do a workshop on "on-site massage". Palmer is considered to be the "father of chair massage" and this was the first time he presented in Canada.

That event probably shaped my massage career more than any other.

I was aghast when I found out he was suggesting that we do short backrubs over the clothing with the client seated. I didn't do "backrubs". I was a paramedical professional!

I was working with our regulatory body, contributing to the Practice of Standards document associated with new legislation that was being enacted. Under the new system we would be regulated under the same regulation that covered medical doctors and other allied health professionals.

I felt it was important to really work at winning the acceptance of the healthcare community and the public at large. If we became more aligned with other healthcare professionals and raised our standards, then people would be more accepting of massage and utilization of massage would increase.

So it was appalling for Palmer to suggest we move backwards and position our services as a relaxation-only service and that we simply do backrubs rather than soft tissue treatment. It seemed like a move back into the dark ages. How would that possibly be beneficial for the industry?

But as I listened to his reasoning, it just made sense. We all love to be touched. It's an innate need and programmed into our nervous system. It's required for our survival. That's why touch is tied into our pleasure centers, just like eating and sex. If you go up behind someone and squeeze their shoulders, how likely are they to say: "Stop! I hate when you do that." It doesn't happen. We need touch and we enjoy it. So why weren't people more accepting of massage and using it more?

It's because there are barriers. To loosely paraphrase Palmer: "To get a massage as we know it, you have to take an hour out of your day to go behind closed doors and get totally naked for a complete stranger who is going to rub greasy oil all over your body and charge you a lot of money for it."

In Palmer's mind, barriers such as fear of the unknown, having to undress, taking an hour or two out of your day, having to travel to your therapist, getting all messy, the high cost, were barriers that prevented people getting massage.

If you remove the barriers, he reasoned, it's only natural that people would make better use of massage.

If people are uncomfortable getting undressed, let them keep their clothes on. If it's not convenient for people to travel to a clinic and get covered in oil, then bring massage to them and don't use oil. If people are afraid of the unknown - who's doing the massage and what they are doing - then do it out in the open and remove the mystery. If massage is too expensive to afford on a regular basis, then shorten up the time frame for a lower per treatment cost.

Chair massage removes all those common barriers that stop people using massage. Not to mention the fact that the very nature of the service removed all the sexual associations that plague this industry.

This was a very different approach to the one I had been pursuing to get massage mainstream. I was trying to make massage acceptable and Palmer was suggesting we make massage accessible. It made perfect sense!

So I bought a chair and immediately started doing chair massage - everywhere! At trade shows, in corporations, hair salons, tanning salons, on the street and even in bars. What was amazing was that any place I did massage could have been a viable business. Even though I was the first doing it in Canada and no one had heard of it, they understood the benefits immediately and used the service.

I focused on the corporate market because it made most sense. I was busy and couldn't do all the seated massage myself. But I could sell large jobs to large corporations and subcontract the work to other therapists for fulfillment. I was very successful. I worked with some of the biggest companies in Canada: IBM, Dell, Nortell, Kelloggs, Levi-Straus, American Express, every major bank, most major financial institutions, most large law firms, hospitals. I sold close to half a million dollars in corporate contracts personally before I passed that business on to someone else on five years later.

If there is anything that will help you become successful at corporate massage, it would be to understand that you are not selling chair massage. Companies don't care about chair massage. However, they do care about their problems. So the key to selling chair massage is identifying problems a company has and proposing a solution that chair massage can provide.

For example, what does a law firm get its administrative staff for Secretaries' Day? Chocolates, monogrammed umbrellas and chocolates are so passé. Chair massage is unique and memorable.

How do you attract attention to your tradeshow booth when you're selling bolts? You offer visitors chair massage at your booth.

How does a financial institution keep its data entry workers happy and on the job as the RRSP deadline hits? You make chair massage available to them through the time of their heaviest workload.

From this perspective, wellness massage is the hardest sale of all. Firstly, when it comes to wellness, there is no pressing problem that needs attention. Secondly, it requires a long-term commitment from the corporation. It's like a marriage. And no company wants to marry you. It's too big a decision and nobody in the organization wants that responsibility. So focus on short-term contracts and events. Those time-limited relationships are more like dating. Dating is easy; marriage is hard. And there's no reason why you can't date the same company multiple times.

My biggest obstacle was getting therapists to fulfill the contracts. Nobody wanted to do chair massage. Therapists had the attitude I had: They were trained paramedical professionals, so why should they do backrubs?

I had no choice but to train my own workforce. At first I did this internally and then I developed an entry-level training program that specialized specifically in chair massage. To this day I teach chair massage workshops and have developed all types of resources, from marketing courses to technique DVDs, to help other therapists incorporate chair massage into their practices. I continue to preach the gospel of chair massage and carry on David Palmer's goal of making massage accessible to the masses and seeing touch become a positive social value.

Creating a "can't fail" mindset...

My clinics did very well. There were some nice synergies between the corporate chair massage I was doing and the clinics. I pulled a fair number of people into the clinics from our work in the field. But that alone wouldn't have been enough to sustain the therapists. I utilized a range of marketing strategies, including some unique strategies that I'll share with you briefly.

Before I do that, however, I want to point out another primary reason for the success of those clinics. This is really a mindset thing. These mindset issues can't be overlooked.

When you have troubles with your business, the issue can be one of two things:

1) You need the knowledge or technical skill to do something. For example, you don't know exactly how to ask someone to rebook because you don't know how to educate your client as to the value of ongoing massage and you don't know what words to use. That's purely a technique issue.

2) You know what needs to be done, but you don't do it. This is where the demons dance in your head and bring up all your personal issues. So you know how to ask someone to rebook, but you don't do it because you're afraid you'll be perceived as needy or you face the possibility of them saying no and rejecting you.

Both issues need to be addressed. It's important to have the knowledge, but you need to have the right mindset to utilize that knowledge. For example, some experts might suggest you charge $150 for an hour of massage and give you specific ways to establish your value. But if you feel like a $40 per hour therapist in your head, you'll never be successful with raising your prices. From this perspective, pricing is really a consciousness issue.

So it's vitally important to shift your mental thinking. In particular, it's important to learn to move from an "I can fail" mindset to an "I can't fail" mindset. And a simple way to do that is simply…

…**treat your business like a client.**

Many therapists who come to my workshops or take my online courses have come to the end of their rope when it comes to marketing their practices. They've tried all kinds of things with limited success and are ready to call it quits. They're fearful of trying anything new because they are afraid that they may fail. They sigh in frustration: "I've tried that and it just doesn't work."

Let's put this in perspective. Imagine you have a client come into your office with some kind of pain complaint. You do your massage and afterwards they tell you that they don't really feel any better. What do you say? "I've tried my massage and it doesn't work. This stupid massage stuff never works. I'll never do that again."

Not likely. But that's the typical response that a therapist is likely to have when their marketing doesn't produce the expected result.

If you are treating a client in this scenario, you'll likely say: "It's taken your body a while to get to its present state and it's going to take some time to get it back to a fully functioning state. Although you didn't seem to respond to the massage today, we'll change our approach and next week we'll focus on these areas." You recognize that they need to go through a process to get better. And they are not always going to see an immediate improvement.

If you've had any training beyond basic relaxation massage, you use a "problem-solving approach to treatment". Whether you know it or not, you take a four-step treatment approach.

1) You assess the client's condition

2) You create a plan of care to help fix the issue

3) You implement your plan: Massage them

4) Then you reassess to see if what you did had any positive effect and you repeat the process

If you didn't reach your goal, then you have to think back through the process to determine what worked and what didn't. Did you fail to assess the problem properly? Was the outcome unrealistic? Was there a problem with your plan or approach? Did you take the necessary actions or did you try to take shortcuts? Go through the process again from Step 1 with this new information.

If you do that consistently with each visit you learn what works and doesn't work. Eventually you narrow down the most effective approaches and before you know it your client is completely healthy and robust.

Now simply translate that process, that strategy, that mindset you are already familiar with, to your business.

1) You need to assess your business realistically. Determine where you are at right now and where you want to be. It's the same process you take with your client.

2) Then you need to develop a plan to get you there. You don't need to have all the answers, just like you don't need to know exactly what is going to work with your client. It's complicated.

3) You don't know what will really work in your particular situation until you implement your plan or take action. That's the next step.

4) Then you reassess your progress. What about your marketing approach worked and what didn't. Try to narrow it down.

Then next time through the process, simply do more of what you determined worked and stop doing the things that don't work. Do that with every marketing effort and you'll soon see your business getting healthier and healthier.

It's a self-correcting approach. For you physiology buffs, it's a negative feedback loop, which is a very positive thing.

So start thinking of your business as a client. Maintain that familiar mindset and you can't possibly fail. Things will just keep getting better and better.

Growing the clinics...

In terms of actual marketing tactics or strategies, I've tested and tracked the results of many: From advertising and direct mail to workshops, PR and networking. I'll mention a couple I think could be useful to almost any therapist.

The first is gift certificates. For many years this was the second largest source of new clients, surpassed only by client referrals.

Like almost every therapist, I had my gift certificates in a drawer behind my front desk. I would sell a limited number of gift certificates, especially around Christmas time. It never occurred to me that these could be a powerful marketing strategy until I got a call from City Hall. They were looking for a gift for employees of one of the departments. They wanted 300 and asked for a discount. I discounted them slightly and made an offer. They felt it was still too expensive and turned it down.

I was disappointed. I could have had 300 new customers without any marketing cost whatsoever. Then I started thinking that it would have likely been worth my while to give those gift certificates away to get new clients. It wouldn't have cost me anything out of pocket to get those clients in my clinic and I knew that my average client at that time was worth about $350 over their buying lifetime. So those 300 City Hall workers would have been worth $105,000 in revenue and that didn't even include revenue from referrals from those customers or gift certificate sales to them.

I don't know about you, but $100,000+ seemed like a fair amount of revenue. And I wouldn't have had to chase those clients down or spend lots of money in advertising to get them. They were actually being sent to me with an implied endorsement by their employer.

I couldn't let the idea of all that lost revenue out of my

head. So I did a test. I gave away 450 gift certificates to a large law firm in the neighborhood. Normally I test things in a small way and as I handed over the gift certificates, I had a small moment of panic. What if all 450 called to redeem their gift certificates at the same time?

What was interesting about this was that the employees were given the half-hour gift certificates without knowing that this was a test. The employees simply thought this was a gift their employer bought them and they had no idea that these were not paid for. There were no catches or strings attached. As an additional bonus, there was an offer on the gift certificate to upgrade to a full hour for an additional fee of just $20.

To my amazement, only about 10% of those 450 certificates were redeemed. That just goes to show you that money is not the greatest barrier preventing people from getting massage.

Out of the ones that were redeemed, 80% upgraded to a full hour. So I made on average $16 for every "free" massage I gave away. As predicted, a very significant percentage rebooked and many continued coming in for massage even years later. If I remember correctly, we made over $13,000 in revenue from those 45 clients – just under $300 per client.

Seeing the benefits of giving gift certificates away, I continued various tests and tracked a number of factors affecting redemption including gift certificate size, color, and expiry date. Armed with this data, I could develop all kinds of offers for discounted gift certificates and could even give them away and know within a small range what my overall profit would be for that campaign.

I went from selling a dozen or so gift certificates at Christmas time to selling hundreds of gift certificates to my clients in holiday promotions.

There are dozens of ways to promote gift certificate sales and I could probably write a small book on the subject. Suffice to say, open up your office drawer, pull out your gift certificates, dust them off and start letting your clients know you have them by displaying them in the treatment rooms and on your reception desk and by simply asking them if they would like to buy them at various holiday times, such as Christmas, Valentine's Day, Mother's Day and Father's Day.

Testing and tracking...

Let me emphasize that this whole process of determining how to effectively sell gift certificates required testing and tracking. This is another key element in successful marketing and is really just an illustration of treating your business like your client.

You should always test out any marketing tactic in a small way. For example, don't commit to advertising somewhere long-term until you've run the ad once to determine whether you got a return on your investment. However, you need to be sure that your test is big enough to give you a meaningful result. Giving away 450 gift certificates to the law firm was probably a bigger test than I needed to do, but giving away 20 or even 50 gift certificates probably wouldn't have given me an accurate indication as to what I could realistically expect.

It's also vitally important to track the financial results of any marketing effort you make. I was able to tag the referral or marketing source in my accounting software, so I could determine exactly how much money I made from any particular expenditure.

For example, I would tag people who came in as the result of my Yellow Page ad and I could determine what my return on investment was for that specific ad. Let's say hypothetically that I spent $900 on my Yellow Page ad for 2002. I could run a report even several years later to look at the total income I received from those clients. Perhaps it was $3,600 in sales. That is a 400% return on investment. That's acceptable, but not great because I have fulfillment costs associated with those massages. I have my therapists to pay, linen, overhead, administration. So at the end of it all I may walk away with $400 in my pocket. It's a lot of risk to walk away with so little money. There are easier ways to make $400.

However, given those objective results, I have the basis to make better decisions and improve the financial returns for my efforts. I have the option to either try a smaller or larger ad, or an ad with different benefit statements, or an ad with color. Again, I can track the results of the new ad to determine whether the changes worked or not. I'll do more of what works - that is, more of what gives me a higher return on investment - and drop the things that don't give me sufficient return. Given this specific scenario, I may choose to drop the Yellow Page ad entirely and spend the $900 on a bulk mail-out to local residents.

Another powerful strategy...

Here's another powerful strategy that is so simple that you'll likely scoff at it. But I've tracked this and I can tell you that it can increase your income by more than 60% even if you don't increase the number of new clients you get each month beyond your usual level. All you have to do is...

...ask your clients to rebook!

Yes, it's that simple. Suggest a specific treatment schedule to them and ask them in a very direct way to book their next appointment. Now there are lots of ways that you can increase the chances of them rebooking, but at some point it all comes down to asking them to book their next appointment.

Personally, I take an assumptive approach. After all, they came to me because they wanted help. They don't know what they need, so it's my ethical obligation to offer my professional opinion, based on my experience, of what kind of treatment schedule they need. And I'll run it past them.

I'll say something like: "Based on our assessment and the pain you're experiencing now, I would suggest you come in twice a week for the next two weeks. You'll probably notice some significant improvement within that timeframe and then I'll have you come in weekly for a few weeks. How does that sound to you?"

Then at the reception desk it's simply a matter of saying: "Why don't we schedule your next appointment for next Thursday at the same time?" Or perhaps: "Let's book your next appointment before you leave because I know you're busy and if you don't do it now we both know it's not going to happen and you really need to get in here."

The bottom line is that you have to ask for the appointment. Your clients are counting on you to take charge and give them recommendations so they can get the results that they want.

A side note on the power of asking…

You really don't know if you'll get something until you ask. At one point, one of my therapists started filling his schedule up with 90-minute treatments. It seemed to happen overnight. He was a busy therapist, but he was always booked for one-hour treatment times. Suddenly, all his treatments turned into 90-minute ones. I had to find out what happened.

"I just thought I'd start asking people if they wanted to do an hour and a half instead of an hour for their next session," he told me. Surprisingly, more than 70% of his clients took him up on the suggestion. His income increased dramatically overnight just because he asked his clients one simple question.

The power of the web...

I eventually sold one of my clinics to a couple of the employees. The university where I had the other clinic saw the profit potential and wanted to take ownership. They tried to cancel my contract. It wasn't worth a legal battle, so I let them buy me out.

When I had my clinics, the internet didn't have the reach it has today. Remember that the browser didn't really exist until about

1995. And for years afterward, dial-up access was so slow that the web never really played a significant role in marketing.

Things have changed dramatically and within the past five years the internet has become a major factor for local businesses. Today, developing a well-optimized website is probably the single most important thing you could do in your practice.

I consider myself an expert in web development and web marketing, including social media. I'm responsible for projects such as Massage Therapy Radio and the World Massage Conference, which is a virtual online conference that had more than 10,000 paid registrants in its first year. Although I'm not a techie by any stretch of the imagination, I understand web marketing: how to get sites ranked, how to develop a strong online presence and, most importantly, how to get visitors to take action and become customers.

Although I didn't get to use the web for marketing my own massage clinics (I sold the clinics before the web was a viable marketing tool), I have since written websites for more than 100 massage therapists. Because I believe in making sure you can measure your return on investment, I set up systems that allowed me to track the results for these websites. I measured visitors to each page, newsletter signups and the number of new clients as a result of the site.

In creating these sites, I used search engine optimization techniques to make sure they were ranked high by the search engines.

Most of these websites were extremely successful as client generating vehicles. They got targeted visitors and, more importantly, they brought in clients. One massage therapist purchased a website as she was graduating from massage school. She was able to completely fill her practice within months from visitors to the website I had created for her. It was so effective that she decided to have another website created for the town right next to hers. When I talked to her more than a year later, she said she was booked out about four weeks in advance.

I know that many therapists say that websites are ineffective at getting clients, but like most marketing, it's all about the way it's done. You don't need anything fancy, but you need a website that is search engine optimized (SEO). This simply means constructing and writing your site in a way that search engines such as Google understand that they should rank your site highly when people are searching for massage in your area.

I know that so-called experts say that you need tons of content, but the reality is that's just not the case and my testing and tracking tells a different story. What you do need is relevant content that the search engines understand.

The search engines are smart. When someone types in "massage tampa" they know that the searcher is likely looking for a massage in Tampa and wants a list of local area massage clinics. If your little five-page brochure site is TampaMassage.com, then Google knows that your site is likely relevant for that searcher. Google will look at the words throughout your site and the links from other websites that point back to your site to confirm that indeed you are a massage business in Tampa. Of course, that's a simplified version of the process. Google takes into consideration more than 100 factors to come up with this determination. But in short, that's how it works.

Whatever you do, don't leave your site in the hands of your 14-year-old son or the neighbor down the street. If you don't invest in doing it right, you can't expect any significant returns from your website. You'll get out of it what you put into it, so make an investment.

If you have the interest and lots of time to go through the learning process, then do it yourself. Otherwise pay someone else to do it for you. It's worth the investment. Even if it costs a couple thousand dollars upfront, the benefits will continue for years and years. If I were a new therapist just coming out of school, I would invest in a website before I even invested in business cards. That's how important I believe it is.

It's also vital to get links that point back to your site. One of the key ways that Google determines that your site should be ranked highly is the number of other sites that have links to yours. So it's very important that you get listed in local online business directories and review sites. Also be sure to post some videos to video-sharing sites, write articles for article directories and submit online press releases.

Social media sites such as Facebook have become extremely popular over the past couple of years. And utilization of these sites is growing exponentially. They provide you with an excellent (and no-cost) way to network with large numbers of people. So it's important to make use of these free online services.

Start by creating a profile page on Facebook if you don't already have one. Facebook allows you to put each contact in a list and you can determine what access each list has to your information. For example, you could create a "family" list and a "massage clients" list. You could give family access to all your information, but at the same time restrict people in your "massage clients" list from accessing your photo albums. Once you get comfortable with Facebook and start building your "friends" list, you can create a Group Page or Fan Page.

It all starts with a website, however, and that should really be the first place you look at investing in marketing your practice.

Final words...

The massage industry is an unusual one in many ways. Massage therapists seem to have a very difficult time seeing their practices as a business. And many seem to have a lot of issues around money.

It's not a bad thing to have a busy successful practice. Your level of income is directly related to the number of lives you touch. Making more money means that you are having a larger impact on your community and bringing the benefits of massage to a larger audience.

Marketing is not bad. It's simply educating the public about the unique benefits you can offer them and helping make use of your massage so they can enjoy those benefits, whether that's relaxation or pain-free living. The better you are at marketing, the larger the impact you can have on your community.

So if I were to give just one piece of advice to you as a massage therapist, it would be to get a marketing education. Reading a book like this where successful therapists share their ideas is a start, but I'd also suggest you take some courses so you can learn how to market your business in a more systematic way. Beyond that, you need to take action on the marketing ideas you learn. Test out various strategies and track your results. Marketing doesn't have to be difficult, but you have to make the investment - of both time and money - to see truly substantial results.

ERIC BROWN BIO

Eric Brown, a massage therapist and educator for over 20 years, is one of the industry's foremost business experts. He provides online business education for massage therapists through BodyworkBiz.com and has created best selling courses, including 60 Clients in 60 Days and Fill Your Practice 101.

Eric is the developer of MassageTherapyRadio.com and co-founder of the World Massage Conference, the largest event in the history of massage. Widely regarded as an expert in chair massage, he has instructional videos available at ChairMassageTechniuqes.com and has a textbook by Pearson Publishing slated for release in 2011.

BodyworkBiz.com

MassageTherapyRadio.com

World Massage Conference.com

"Luck is the by-product of busting your fanny."

- Don Sutton

2

LAURA ALLEN

Massage therapy is my second career. For about 25 years, I was a chef and restaurant owner. One day, I looked at my husband, and said: "I've cooked 875,000 meals, and I'm done." The day I made this magnanimous decision, I really didn't know what I was going to do ... but I'm the type who has to stay busy. If I won the lottery, I'd still have to work. I'm not happy sitting around.

It so happened that the owner of a massage school frequented my restaurant. I sat down at her table and told her I was selling out - and I asked her for a job. I told her I could type, file, or sweep the floor. I really wanted some kind of mindless job that meant that I wouldn't have to work 100 hours a week any more as I had in the restaurant. She told me she was looking for someone to work in her office, so a couple of weeks later - after I had sold out my half of the restaurant to my partner - I went to work at The Whole You School of Massage & Bodywork. The second day I was there, I impulsively enrolled in the weekend massage program at the school. In a moment of insanity, I also went back to college to get a degree in psychology. So I worked during the day, went to school at night and on the weekends, and I ultimately ended up working there as the administrator and an instructor for five years before leaving to open my own clinic.

In a twist of fate, the owner of the school, who had been the first massage therapist in at least a 50-mile radius in our town, had also been the one to give me my first massage years before, when I had woken up one morning with my neck so stiff I couldn't move it, and my mother took me to get a massage. I walked out an hour later with my full range of motion restored, and that made a believer (and a client) out of me.

About five years before I got out of the restaurant business, a friend asked me to go to a class called "Healing Touch." She said she had to take a partner, and she would pay if I would go. I didn't know what Healing Touch was, but I was amazed when I attended the class. For the next five years, right up until my enrollment in massage school, I used it on friends and family, the dog, and anyone who would sit still long enough. So it really wasn't much of a jump into the world of massage. Besides, I saw all these people coming into the clinic at the school ... people who looked stressed out and in pain, and then an hour or so later walking out feeling so much better. I thought it had to be the best job in the world to be able to help people like that. I was ready. Switching gears and going into the massage profession has been the best move I've ever made.

While I was still employed at the school, I noticed the students there were complaining about the test-prep books that were available. I had always enjoyed writing and had written several articles for magazines, so I thought I'd just write a book to address the students' complaints that there wasn't enough pathology or Eastern medicine in the books that were already out there. It took me three months to write it, and I had 50 copies printed at our local print shop. They sold out. The book was pitiful, too. I didn't have it professionally edited, and there weren't any illustrations in it. It was just straight information.

About that time, Lippincott Williams & Wilkins sent a letter to the massage school looking for teachers to review manuscripts. I filled out the application, and one of the questions on it was: "Have you ever published anything?" I wrote in the title of my self-published book. A few weeks later, I received a letter asking me to send them a copy. I did, and a few weeks later, they sent me a letter asking for seven copies to send out to reviewers. I responded, and a couple of months later, I received a phone call from their acquisitions editor saying congratulations, they'd like to publish my book, the *Plain & Simple Guide to Therapeutic Massage & Bodywork Examinations*. I was beside myself, especially when they flew me up to their offices in Baltimore and put me up in a ritzy hotel overlooking the harbor. The next day, I met with their editors, signed the official contract, and got to work turning my book into a real book ... they considered my pitiful little self-publication to be the first draft.

Within a couple of years, it was made a required text in about 100 schools. The second edition was released in 2009. In 2008, LWW published my second book, *One Year to a Successful Massage Therapy Practice*. The way that book came about is a whole other story.

In 2003, a couple of massage therapists we knew asked my husband and me to go into business with them. They had already scoped out a new professional building that had been built downtown, and decided it was a good location. We agreed. It had its own parking lot, a big plus in our town. I gave a month's notice at the massage school, and got to work at the new place, which we named THERA-SSAGE. Two months later, the couple decided they wanted out. Their parting words were that they could see that this business was never going to support four people. Today it supports 14 and has necessitated taking over two adjoining suites of offices. We've added a chiropractor, a professional clinical herbalist, an acupuncturist, an RN trained in aesthetics and manual lymphatic drainage, and the rest are massage therapists.

The turning point in the business actually occurred the day after the partners left. One of the doctors in town came to the office and purchased 26 gift certificates - one for every member of his group practice's staff. If I needed a sign from the universe that everything was going to work out great, that was it.

My husband is a talented carpenter and builder, employed by a general contractor. For years our phone had been ringing off the hook with people wanting him to do jobs on the side, and I had been encouraging him to strike out on his own. He decided to take that plunge about the same time we opened the clinic ... so there we were - both of us used to drawing a regular salary, and suddenly both self-employed, not knowing for sure if we'd have two nickels to rub together. We joked about the fact that it's a good thing we enjoy eating a lot of rice and beans, because it was all we could afford.

I needed to promote the business, but I didn't have enough money to do the kind of substantial advertising that most start-ups need to do. So I started thinking of things to do to get the word out, without spending money. No-cost and low-cost marketing strategies have been the backbone of my advertising plan since the day I opened, and they continue to be. Here are some of my favorites that have been successful:

- The Humble Flyer: There are bulletin boards in every community, in numerous places. I print flyers in neon colors to attract attention, and they're all over the county. For example, there's a community college three miles away. They have a bulletin board in every hallway. My flyer is on every single one of them.

- The Two-Cards-a-Day Plan: I make it a point to give my business card to two new people every single day. It might be a frazzled mother trying to grocery shop with three kids in tow, or a business person I meet at a community event, but the point **is**, just do it!

- The Two-fer: Two massages for the price of one. Why would you do that? Because you will stipulate that one of the recipients must be a new client - and that it's someone who lives in the area. This rewards an existing client for bringing in a referral, and introduces someone new to your business. Offer it during a slow period when business is down.

- Press Releases: It's been an ongoing goal of mine to get my name in the news at least once a month for free - through the use of press releases. Send out the first one when you graduate from massage school. Use a press release to announce that you're employed somewhere new, that you've attended continuing education or a convention, that you're hosting a health fair or an open house ... any newsworthy opportunity. Business editors are actively seeking news about the people in their communities.

• Maximize What You Have: Your brochures aren't doing that much good if they're just sitting in a holder in your office, available only to the people who are already in there. Always carry some with you! Take them to your county's tourism center. Hotels always have lobby racks for brochures. If you belong to the Chamber of Commerce, they always have a place for displaying the literature of member businesses. Realty offices often have them as well - they want people moving into the community to see what local attractions, goods and services are available.

• Social Networking: If you're not participating, why not? It's free. A Facebook Fan Page for your business, a personal presence on LinkedIn, MySpace, Ning networks, and anywhere that you can use to establish an internet presence and links for yourself and your business are definitely worth taking advantage of.

- Your Website: If you still don't have one, it's time to move out of the Dark Ages. The public *expects* businesses to have a web presence nowadays. You can not only educate the public about your business, you can also sell gift certificates online and book appointments online as well.

- Cultivate Relationships with Realtors: I have cultivated relationships with realtors because they meet everyone new coming into town, and I make sure they have plenty of my cards. In fact, I have had special cards made for my realtor buds that say "You must be a VIP if you're with Scott Walker from Century 21" and it gets them $10 off their first visit here.

- Cross-Referrals: People who are new to town are always needing a plumber, a carpenter, a doctor, or someone to cater their daughter's wedding. I have the cards of everyone from accountants to window-washers alphabetized by their profession. When I give out someone else's business card, I write "Tell them Laura Allen from THERA-SSAGE sent you" on the back of it.

The first year I was in business, we took in the princely sum of $16,000. The second year, that was multiplied by five. The fifth year, we cracked $300,000. And it continues to grow every year, including during the recession, during which our county had the second highest unemployment rate out of the 100 counties in North Carolina and the 13th worst in the nation.

I realized that all the little things I was doing to build the business would make a great book to help other therapists, so I started writing it. I had a meeting with the folks from LWW to discuss a book on Swedish massage that they had asked me to write. LWW publishes a lot of massage books, and that's a convenient place to meet up with all their authors. So I walked into the meeting, placed the pile in front of the Big Guy, and said: "Here are the first nine chapters, and I hate to tell you that I am not at all excited about this book. But let me tell you what I am excited about!" Before he could say a word, I launched into a pitch for my *One Year to a Successful Massage Therapy Practice* book. When I finally shut up, he and the rest of the editors around the table just burst out laughing and kind of went "Okay". The contract was signed just a couple of weeks later.

My third book is, *A Massage Therapist's Guide to Business.* I've tried to impart practical advice based on my experiences ... and you always learn a lot in the school of hard knocks! One of the most important lessons about where and how to market your business **is to** take a good look at ROI - return on investment - when you're deciding where, and how much money to spend on advertising. We're bombarded every day with marketing "opportunities". And when you're new and just starting out in business, it's tempting to advertise anywhere and everywhere. Ideally, though, you want to spend your money where you're going to get the biggest bang for your buck. Let's say you could purchase a $200 ad in *Carolina Woman Magazine,* which has a circulation of 5,000 people - and the primary audience is women - which is okay, if that's the population you want to reach. Or, you purchase a $200 ad in the local newspaper, which has a circulation of 35,000 people of every type. It doesn't take a rocket scientist to figure out which one is the better choice.

If your child asks you to buy an ad on the Little League calendar, naturally you're not going to refuse your child. But if it isn't your child putting the guilt trip on you, consider the ROI. The Little League calendar will be seen by the parents of the Little Leaguers, and not many others. If you have the money to spare, you should certainly support any and every organization you want to by buying ad space ... the church cookbooks, the play programs, and so forth. But just bear in mind, if you only have a certain amount to spend, when you spend it in one place, you don't have it to spend somewhere else that might have been more effective for you.

I write regularly for *Massage & Bodywork, Massage Magazine,* and *Massage Today.* I am also known for blogging about the politics of the massage therapy profession. I teach marketing and professional ethics, among other things, to massage therapists. I'm fortunate enough to be on the faculty of a massage school in Ireland, the home of my heart and my ancestors, and I travel there every year to teach. In just the past few weeks, I've been to six different states to teach. I love what I do and I do what I love.

When I was growing up, my parents instilled in me the belief that I could do whatever I wanted to do. Then, for a time in my twenties, I fell in love with the wrong person, and went down the path of being in an abusive marriage. I got out alive, but it took some time for me to round up any self-esteem. I had been told over and over that I was nobody and wouldn't ever be anybody. I heard it so many times I started to believe it. Today, I am happy with who I am. I am married again to a wonderful person who supports my plans and dreams instead of shooting them down. When it comes to your own hopes and dreams, you want to have positive people around you who will support that. If someone nay-says your plan to become a massage therapist, or to go into business for yourself, consider the source. Is the person who's being negative a successful person? Or is it someone who's unhappy with their own situation and who just doesn't want to support *anything* if it doesn't have to do with them? Seek out mentors who will be a support system for you - and who can also give you a reality check when you need one. And we all do, from time to time.

I would suggest to new therapists starting out that the biggest mistake you can make is sitting by the phone waiting for business to come to you. Instead, go out and get it. Introduce yourself to at least two new people every day and give them your business card. Network with other therapists and the other business people in your community. Get involved and stay involved! Once you start getting some success, don't think it's okay to rest on your laurels. I devote 30 minutes every morning to marketing my business. That might mean calling people we haven't seen lately, working up a new ad or promotion, sending out "Welcome to our practice" cards, or any other thing designed to grow our business.

The idea of success is unique and relative. Some therapists may want something similar to what I've built; some people may want six clients a week, plenty of time off to go fishing, and no one to worry about except themselves. As long as you get whatever it is that you want, you're being successful - even if that doesn't fit everybody's picture.

One other piece of advice I have is to take care of yourself. Doing yoga, Tai Chi, dancing, playing sports, or whatever recreation feels good to you - do it and do it consistently. Pace yourself; leave yourself plenty of time in between appointments to regroup, and don't do so many people in one day that your butt drags out the door 10 minutes behind the rest of you. The most important sermon I can preach is to get regular massage! We can't stand there and tell clients they need regular massage when we're not taking care of ourselves. Burn-out comes along when we don't look out for number one. I've never suffered a moment of that, because I get on the table and let someone take care of me at least a couple of times a month. If I'm feeling especially needy, I might get three in a week. I just can't do without it. I also spend a few minutes in meditation every morning and every evening. I subscribe to Deepak Chopra's definition of meditation. He says: "Prayer is when you are talking to God and asking for something. Meditation is when you are sitting quietly listening to what He has to say."

I also encourage you not to give up. I see many therapists - in fact, many businesses of other kinds too - set up shop and a year later they've gone out of business. Don't do that! It takes a while to get established, and it takes capital to operate a business until the money starts flowing in. Plan carefully. Write a business plan before you set out into the world of entrepreneurship. Stay on top of your finances and your record-keeping. If you're not good at balancing your checkbook, admit that and get someone to help you before you find yourself overdrawn and crying at the bank.

Set goals and work for them. My goal, since the day I opened my business, has been to get one new client every day, 365 days a year. Since we're closed on Sunday, that means we have to get two on some other day. I'm glad to say that we have cracked that goal every single year. I have a sign with the magic number hanging on my bulletin board where I have to see it every day. I don't keep my goals for my business to myself; I share them with my staff and they get just as excited as I do when I report how close we are to the goal, or when we've actually met one. It gives me something to work for and something to look forward to. Give up thinking you're going to do so-and-so "someday." Set a definite goal and a timeline and put a plan out there to make it happen. We have the best job in the world - helping people to feel better - and we deserve to prosper, but it doesn't happen by accident. It happens when you plan for it.

LAURA ALLEN BIO

Laura Allen is a massage therapist, educator, and author of Plain & Simple Guide to Therapeutic Massage & Bodywork Examinations (2nd ed, LWW, 2010), One Year to a Successful Massage Therapy Practice (LWW, 2008) and Massage Therapist's Guide to Business (LWW, 2011).

Laura Allen

THERA-SSAGE

431 S. Main Street, Suite 2

Rutherfordton, NC 28139

(828) 288-3727

www.thera-ssage.com

www.lauraallenmt.com

www.educatedheart.com

"There came a time when the risk to remain tight in the bud was more painful than the risk it took to blossom."

\- Anaïs Nin

3

ANN ROSS

My desire to become a massage therapist literally came about through a dream at the age of 24. A message was conveyed to me that, had I not been listening, would have meant passing up a beautiful gift handed to me at the ideal time in my life. Becoming a massage therapist was my third career change and was definitely the epitome of "third time's a charm". I had no idea that becoming a massage therapist was my destiny, or that it would change my life the way that it has. Where would I be if I hadn't found this profession? I can't say. What I can say is that it saved me from myself at the most significant time in my life, and quite possibly kept me from a life full of emptiness, had it not graced me with its presence. Becoming a massage therapist shifted me from being an insecure young woman full of self-doubt, and propelled me into the life full of promise, fulfillment, happiness and confidence I know today. It's funny how when you stop and just "listen" to the silence, you will find the answers. They don't always come right away, but will always show their face at just the right time. I listened, I took action, I grew and I transformed! This story is my true path of insecurity, disappointment, failure, transformation, self-acceptance and, finally, finding my place in the world through this beautiful field of massage therapy. If I can do it, anyone can!

My professional life up until the point of becoming a massage therapist had been empty, unfulfilled and a complete disappointment. My entire life had been spent with a steady feeling of insecurity and a huge lack of self-confidence. While I had always been an outgoing, fun-loving child, I carried around the heavy weight of anxiety, insecurity and the feeling that I was never quite good enough. This feeling followed me through high school graduation and into my early adulthood, where I got completely lost in the search of "what next?" and "who am I?". My entire life, all I had heard was "there is no money for college". Talking about the future or a career was something that was never discussed in my home. As long as I graduated high school with good grades and received a diploma, that was what mattered. I never knew myself enough past my insecurities to think long-term or **to** know what I was passionate about. So, I did the most logical thing for myself after high school graduation... I enrolled in cosmetology school. I figured that if I was going to do something with my life, I might as well learn a skill that was focused, fast and had great income potential. I was never fond of the idea of college anyway. Something about taking required classes that didn't interest me just seemed like wasted time. Honestly, it sounded like more high school to me. No thanks! The 1,800 hours I spent in cosmetology school in my first year out of high school were challenging, exciting and a huge part of who I am today.

However, after just three years in the profession I walked away from everything I had worked so hard for and changed my career. I had allowed myself to be sucked into the dream of working for a well-known, prestigious salon and the possibilities of happiness and excitement I thought it would provide me. As a 19-year-old woman, working for the best-known salon in the Seattle area seemed like a dream come true. Or so I thought! After just a few weeks of working for this company, I knew I had made a bad decision. I was working myself to death every day and had just a few pennies to show for it at the end of the month. In addition, I didn't fit in with my co-workers, I never felt pretty or trendy enough to work there and I didn't agree with the fundamental business practices of the company at the time. Even though, looking back, leaving that company was one of the healthiest decisions I have ever made for myself, at the time I was devastated that it didn't work out. I felt like a complete failure, my insecurity level was at an all-time high and I was severely disheartened. But I couldn't escape the truth: I had fallen out of love with what I was doing for a living. The emptiness I felt as I went to work each day was unbearable and I knew it was time to move on. Like a romantic relationship that didn't work out the way I had hoped, it was time to say goodbye.

So at the age of 21 I had just quit my first profession and was again searching for happiness and fulfillment in the occupational arena. I was hired as a customer service representative for a wireless company and surprisingly fell in love with this job. I loved that I could just go to work each day, do my job and leave. I enjoyed the people I worked with and was really good at what I did.

After just a year I was promoted to work on a team that handled back-end project work for corporate accounts. I was really enjoying my life at this point. But, as I started to look at my future with this company, something just didn't sit right with me. The company was great, but my income potential was extremely limited. Even if I became a manager, the idea of a salary that would cap off at a certain point just didn't seem right. Not to mention that after just a few years of doing this kind of work, I missed the fulfillment of doing something that actually mattered. I missed helping people on a deep level.

As I became more and more bored with my life, I began to lose direction and got lost in the day-to-day mundane. I would go home at night, sit on the couch and sink into my unhappiness. I began going out after work just to have something to do. I was surrounding myself with people who weren't bringing anything to my life and that scared me. Something was off, my life was vacant and I was fearful of the lonely, empty feelings that consumed my every day. I couldn't imagine that the rest of my life was going to feel this way. Something had to change… and fast!

And so it did change, in the blink of an eye. I woke one morning from a dream and kept hearing the words "massage therapy". It was like somebody had lit a flame inside my soul that was incapable of being destroyed. I was alive with the excitement and promise of a fulfilled life through massage therapy. I can't describe it in words; it was just a feeling inside of me that made sense, a gift that was sent to me. All I had to do was open my heart and listen to the message. The message was clear: "Massage therapy will lead you to a life of fulfillment, positive challenges, abundance and inner peace."

I enrolled in massage school a week later and started a few months after that. I quickly realized that my education in the massage therapy profession was going to be so much more than I could have ever imagined. Call me naïve, but I really thought I was going to school to learn techniques to give a good massage, not the origins, insertions and attachments for each muscle. Nor did I realize I was going to be learning the mechanics of body movement and muscle imbalances. I was blown away by how "medical" everything I was learning seemed. But, for the first time in my life, the challenges that school presented in front of me no longer exaggerated my insecurities. On the contrary, school was a welcome challenge for me. It just felt right! I fell in love almost immediately with massage therapy. The art of touch came naturally to me and I enjoyed my curriculum. Because I was already accustomed to touch and being close to people due to my cosmetology experience, my teachers often commented on my confidence and sense of poise.

School didn't come without sacrifice, though. I worked full-time during the days at my wireless desk job and went to school in the evenings. It was an exhausting year! One thing that most people don't know about me is that while I was in school and up until the time I graduated, I never considered starting my own business. It was my intention the entire time that I was in school to graduate and begin work at a spa. I saw myself leaving my desk job on graduation and working full-time at a high-end spa, providing spa treatments and relaxation massage. Never in a million years would I believe that I would become the successful, self-employed massage therapist that I am today. It took just a few, simple words of encouragement from a mentor to change all of that for me.

I was nearing graduation and had a required meeting with my graduate services coordinator. I owe everything to this wonderful woman and the words of encouragement she said to me that day. We were discussing my plans after graduation and she handed me the information to register for my business license. I casually said to her: "Oh, don't worry about giving me the information for that, I'm just going to be working at a spa." She looked at me with a puzzled expression and said: "You mean you're not going to work for yourself?" "No," I said. "I don't want to deal with the stress of taxes and stuff." She had a confused look on her face. I wasn't sure where this was going and I was starting to get a little nervous. What was the issue here? What is so wrong about wanting to work for a spa? She looked me straight in the eye and said: "Ann, if ANYONE can open their own business and be successful at it, it's you!" "Really?" I said. Nobody had EVER said anything like that to me before. Nobody! Up until that point in my life, I had never, even for one second, had so much as a thought about becoming self-employed. It just wasn't in my vocabulary, or my life plan.

I come from a family of hard working employees and was programmed at a young age to think only in terms of finding a job. Bless my parents' heart because they instilled a good, strong work ethic that is deep-rooted in me. But everything up until that point in my life had been about average choices, running away from my insecurities, finding a job and standing in the background. Starting my own business meant putting myself out there, pushing through my fears and taking a risk, something I wasn't sure I was able to handle. But there was something in the way she looked at me and spoke to me that day. Something she said stuck with me and I left there with anticipation and eagerness about starting my own business.

I graduated from school and got my massage license shortly after. During this time I was still working at my desk job. I kept the idea of self-employment in the back of my head, but began applying for available spa jobs. I was still afraid and wasn't quite sure if starting my own business was something I would be able to do, so I thought I would look for work as an employee and see what happened. The application process wasn't easy, though. I began realizing that most wouldn't hire me because of my lack of experience. I did end up going for one interview at a well-known spa, hoping and praying before **it** even started that I would get hired. The first part of the interview was a tour of the salon and spa. After that, we sat down and went over the commission structure and my potential future income. Yikes! I did the math in my head and quickly realized that if I was consistently booked (which I knew was nearly impossible), my income would cap out at around the rate I was making at my desk job (around $2,500 per month after taxes). This rate did not include any income from tips. It was just the commission structure. Even then though, it scared me to think that if I wanted to make a decent living, it was going to be through the tips I received, not the commission pay. Not to mention that financial growth didn't even seem possible. But I wanted to leave my desk job so badly and start my career as a massage therapist. I was desperate! So, I scheduled a practical interview for the following week. Over the next few days I couldn't shake this uneasy feeling I was having about the pay structure and my future because of it. It was then that I realized that all signs were pointing to self-employment. It was time to accept that I was destined to be a business-owner and own my future. I cancelled my interview with the spa and never looked back.

A month after that, I applied for my state business license and became an official small business owner. I had no idea what I was getting myself into! Again, I was desperate and began seeking a space to run my business out of anywhere and everywhere. I was looking in tanning salons, hair salons and any place that seemed like an option. I had absolutely no direction or any idea of who I was as a business owner. All I knew was that I was a massage therapist who needed a space to provide massage in. After a month I was blessed to find space in a women's fitness club just five minutes from my daytime desk job. The space was perfect. I could continue to work during the day at my desk job, and provide massage in the evenings. The owner was a lovely, kind woman and did everything she could to fill my appointment book. Looking back at that early time in my career, I was still locked into the "employee mindset" and expected her to bring me work. I became frustrated that I was doing only four-six massages per month after six months and began to get worried. When I look back at myself during this time, I can't help but see all of the mistakes I was making. I had no clue what I was doing and expected everything to happen for me simply because I had a business license and a place to provide massage. That was my biggest mistake at the time and to this day, one of the biggest mistakes I see other massage therapists making. But how are we to always know, or realize, this if we haven't been educated or haven't gone through some of the mistakes it takes to learn this? If all you have been is an employee, how do you know how to think like a business owner? How do you even know that the shift from employee to employer must happen? I certainly didn't know it. Nobody told me that it needed to happen. I stumbled upon this realization on my own simply by experiencing challenges and taking accountability for myself. This was a poignant time in my life and a turning point in my career.

The next phase of my career happened quickly and would turn out to be the beginning of many events that led me to the successful business owner I am today. I was speaking one day with a family friend who also happened to be a massage therapist and she offered to share her space with me at a chiropractic clinic in Seattle. Everything up until that moment in my career had been about not wanting to work in the "medical" side of our profession. I was afraid of insurance companies, medication, injuries, doctors, and everything that came with clinical work. I had always said that working with or for a chiropractor was the last thing I wanted to do, hence the reason for seeking employment at a spa. But here was that feeling inside of me again, telling me that this was going to be the opportunity that I needed that would change everything. I made the decision to leave the women's fitness club and began renting the space in the chiropractic clinic three days a week.

Again, I continued to work during the day at my desk job so that my income would remain steady and secured. It was my intention to remain working there until my clientele was built up enough to support me financially. At this point I had already been graduated from school for a year and felt like I was starting all over again. Flash forward a few months and I was in the same position as before: one or two clients a week here and there. I couldn't believe that I was in the same position again! Working here was supposed to be my big break and for some reason it wasn't happening. I was frustrated and really scared that this was never going to happen for me. I wanted so badly to leave my day job and get on with my life but I was so far from that ever happening. I was starting to doubt if it was ever going to happen.

I'm not sure exactly what it was that led me to the realization that would change things for me, but the awareness of it was huge and life-changing. I don't recall the exact moment, but I do recall the awareness of myself, taking accountability for myself, my future, my career, my business and the idea that if I didn't start turning things around, I was forever going to be unhappy with my life. I was done playing the victim with my career and I was ready to make things happen. It was time to take responsibility for myself and my life. No more excuses!

The very first step I took was to get educated. I began researching business ownership, marketing, client attraction and everything that involved growing a business. My school didn't necessarily do a great job at preparing us for business ownership. But I wasn't going to let that stop me. I was on fire with the idea that I could really make this work this time. I was on the verge of success and was eager to begin my journey. I remember asking a colleague her opinion regarding spending money on courses about growing a successful business. Her words were: "Oh, don't waste your money, you don't need that." Her thought was that I could just build my business off referrals. A great idea for sure, but you need clients to build a business on referrals. "How do you get the darn clients?" I kept thinking. I'm so thankful I didn't take her advice! Something inside of me knew that it was important to educate myself and to spend money learning the fundamentals of success and client attraction. I began reading every book and course I could get my hands on. The very first course I bought online was one of the scariest moments for me. A man by the name of Todd Brown had become a well-known marketing expert for massage therapists. He was consistently helping thousands of therapists across the country build successful businesses for themselves and I wanted a piece of the pie. His course "Mega Success System for Massage Therapists" wasn't cheap and I remember being terrified as I made my purchase that day. I was so excited when my course came in the mail and I immediately sat down and began reading the enormous manual. Each chapter I read through helped me understand the concepts of client attraction, direct response marketing and unique selling propositions. I was finally understanding the concepts of effective marketing and massage business ownership.

It's funny, because I don't remember necessarily implementing any particular thing he taught. What I do remember is that through all of my self-education and through the thousands of dollars I spent on courses, the shift in my mindset from employee to business owner magically appeared. I was no longer the victim in a sluggish business. I had become a go-getter, an innovator and a business owner excited about my future. I began thinking outside the box, taking the things I was learning and making them my own. I was putting my own spin on things and being creative in a way that was branding me. I started seeing results and attracting clients into my practice at a shocking rate. I went from nought to two clients a week to six to 12 clients a week in only three to six months.

I will admit, my success came into my life when I started doing things that were uncomfortable to me. I was terrified of billing insurance companies, but decided to become a contracted provider because I knew that I would have an enormous amount of exposure if I did. Everything I heard about working with insurance companies was negative, but I wasn't going to let that stop me. Also, I knew nothing about the internet, but created my own website that branded me, my expertise in the field and the unique qualities that made me special. My website was more than just an online brochure - it glorified me, without being conceited. It was my special online real estate that allowed potential clients to see into the world of massage therapy, through me as their confidante and specialist. My website was one of the most important aspects of my success. Not only was it uncommon for therapists to have websites at the time, but mine was different. It spoke to potential clients and made them feel safe. After reading my website they wanted to book an appointment with me. In addition, I began offering a complimentary 30-minute session (with the option to upgrade at a cost) as an opportunity for potential clients to meet me, get to know me and receive a sample of my unique session without the worry of money out of their pocket. It was an exclusive, risk-free offer that attracted a great deal of clients into my practice. Again, this was something that most therapists were not doing at the time and it allowed me to get my hands on as many people as possible and help build the trust that potential clients are looking for in a massage therapist. In addition, I created alliances with other healthcare professionals and business owners. I was terrified of getting to know other therapists, physicians, attorneys and chiropractors. I saw them as being "better than" or "superior to" me. I was severely insecure and lacked the confidence I knew was important if I was going to make it. But I didn't want to come across as scared, insecure or unsure of myself. So, I learned to fake my confidence on the outside very well and in a short time my external "fake" confidence had shifted into a reality for me. And lastly, I made it my mission and number one priority to give the utmost care to my clients. I positioned myself as part of their healthcare team, advising each person that I am more than just an hour of "pampering" and that I am dedicated to their wellbeing. I wanted people to understand that massage is an important part of their health and wellness. I wanted to remove the guilt that so many have associated with receiving massage. In addition to being a source of health in their lives, I always went out of my way to provide impeccable quality and customer service at all times. I organized my business in such a way that I was able to run things smoothly and create a sense of ease in doing business with me. I greatly value the fact that each person is choosing to spend his or her money with me, in a city where there are many massage therapists. I want my clients to feel appreciated, taken care of and always valued. It was this combination of skills and mindset that ultimately led to my success as a self-employed massage therapist.

Excitedly, within a year of shifting myself and pushing through these fears, boundaries and taking responsibility for myself, I was finally free from my daytime desk job, the job that I had been doing for seven years of my life. The job that supported me through massage school and starting my own business was no longer a part of my life. Less than two years after beginning my journey as a self-employed massage therapist, I was officially a full-time, successful massage therapy business owner. It was both an exciting time in my life and so incredibly terrifying. On one hand, I had officially made the leap to being a full-time massage therapist, my dream come true.

On the other hand, I no longer had the crutch of my day job to fall back on. This was on me now! It was my fear of failure that pushed me forward and kept me on my path of success. I continued to invest in my education and myself, and hustled on a constant basis to keep my business going strong.

I spent the next two years growing my business at the chiropractic clinic and loving every minute of it. It was during those two years that I began to dream about the possibility of helping other massage therapists someday. I wasn't sure exactly how to go about it, I just knew that someday it would make a great addition to my already successful business. I had so much to share and didn't want other therapists to struggle the way I had. I felt I had all the answers! In addition, this was a pivotal time in my career because I began to understand the importance of earning an income through my body. This actually scared me. If I got sick, hurt or couldn't work, I didn't get paid. I was starting to realize that it wasn't smart or safe to rely on one source of income, especially through the use of my body. Yes, massage therapists can make a great living just by providing massage, I am proof of that. But is it realistic to put all of your eggs in one basket? Should we be relying on our bodies as our only source of income? It's this realization that led me to seek out other streams of income, even though I was the owner of a successful small business. It had only been about a year that I was doing massage full-time, but I was starting to think outside the box. Who said I had to make all of my money through massage? I was self-employed now. I could make money doing whatever I wanted!

During this time I was introduced to the concept of network marketing, as well as affiliate marketing. I was doing some research online one evening and found an entire world where people were earning a great living online through network marketing. This wasn't the scammy type of businesses that exist on the internet. Nor was it the "beg your family and friends" type of business. This was a classy and professional business model that was very appealing to me. I began studying this profession and the notion of owning a business through the internet. It was 2008 and the concept of social media was beginning to take the internet by storm. After much research and anticipation, I became involved with a network marketing company. This company, a 12-year-old biotech, had just launched its customized DNA, plant and whole food-based nutritional supplements and skincare to the marketplace. Being the healthcare provider that I was, becoming an independent affiliate for this company just made sense. The concept of network marketing was a little new and overwhelming for me at first, but through my education I now have the knowledge that allows me to earn monthly commissions through this company by offering the product to my clients, as well as offering a business opportunity to other healthcare providers and those seeking self-employment. It has been an amazing addition to my massage practice.

It was through becoming an independent affiliate in network marketing that my education in the field of websites, online marketing, and the future of business ownership grew. Had I not reached out and taken the chance to learn on my own terms, I might not have known how to adapt to the always changing world of the internet. The internet is an enormous element now of the way people do business, customers and owners alike. It's important to always be educating yourself as the times change, even if it's not always directly related to our field of massage therapy.

In addition to educating myself and expanding my income potential through other business models, my massage therapy practice was continuing to grow. It was late summer 2008, I had been doing massage therapy full-time for only two years and I began searching for a place to open my own business. I hadn't anticipated leaving the chiropractic clinic so soon, but knew that it was time. I wanted more freedom with my space, my time and I wanted to offer my clients the opportunity to receive a massage from me in a space that was entirely my own. This time I knew the importance of finding the "perfect" place. Unlike the first time around, I was no longer desperate and I understood the need to present myself and my business from a new perspective. I spent weeks looking for the right place and was blessed when I found a brand-new, gorgeous studio space just five miles from the chiropractic clinic. I customized the space to my liking by building a private room and decorating it in a style that is calming, modern and simple. I was a bit scared to leave the space at the chiropractic clinic and the certain flow of referrals I had been exposed to for the last three years, but I knew in my heart that it was time to step it up a notch. It was again that feeling inside of me that presented itself, saying that this was right and everything would work out beautifully.

It was November 4 2008 and I was open for business in my new location! My schedule was booked out into December already and I couldn't believe it. I had been running specials for my existing clients to thank them for their patronage and to give them an incentive to come see my new place. I knew if it wasn't for them, I wouldn't be able to open my own location - something I always remind myself of and never take for granted. So many of my clients took full advantage of my specials during that time, that I generated thousands of dollars in revenue those first two months. It was an exciting time in a new chapter in my career. I was the official owner of a small business location and my client base was continuing to expand. Because my studio sits in a community among other small business owners with its own store-front window, in a safe neighborhood with a generous amount of foot traffic, I have attracted a number of new clients by people walking by. Talk about free advertising!

Within a few months of opening my studio, I began looking for massage therapists who were interested in renting my space on my days off. I knew that I only wanted to work four days per week and could bring in some income by sharing my space the other three days. Since opening my studio, I have had at least one therapist renting from me at all times, sometimes two. During this time in my life and career, the thought of hiring an employee felt like a daunting, unappealing idea. Hiring a subcontractor to rent my space allowed me to earn extra money without the responsibilities that come with employees.

It was also during this time that I shifted my work schedule into one that better suited me. I had been seeing 25-30 clients per week, working late mornings, afternoons, evenings and Saturdays through the years and it was starting to take its toll on me. I modified my schedule to allow for 20 clients per week, leaving the office by 5pm and still working on Saturdays. This has allowed me to take better care of myself so that I can be a healthy, thriving massage therapist. Yes, I lost some clients, but most adapted to my new schedule by leaving work early, getting a massage on their lunch break and scheduling in advance on Saturdays.

As 2009 progressed, I became hungry again with the notion of becoming a mentor for massage therapists searching for direction in their career. After six years in the field, I felt it was finally time to take my knowledge and offer it to those in need. I knew so much about creating a successful business and felt it wouldn't be right to keep this crucial information to myself. I knew I could have used someone like myself when I was starting out. I wanted nothing more than to be a positive source of motivation, empowerment and education for massage therapists. But it was important before doing any kind of teaching or mentoring that I first prove to myself that I could be a leader. I didn't want to just go out there and start talking about stuff before I knew for sure that what I was teaching was valid and valuable. 2009 proved to be the year that I found the confidence in myself to reach new heights. I had shown myself first and foremost that I was capable of growing a business from scratch without any level of knowledge. I had learned everything on my own initiative and applied my knowledge in a way that proved fruitful. It was time to take it forward. However, I was terrified of putting myself out there, knowing that people would be judging me, good and bad. My insecurities once again resurfaced and I found myself putting things off and making excuses. There was that pesky fear showing itself again! Just as in the past, I knew that fear was, in fact, my friend and that it was time to push through and go for it. I finally launched my blog Massage Marketing Mentor in December 2009 and held my breath waiting for massage therapists to walk through my online door. I began writing blog posts, making videos and creating free training. I poured my heart and soul into my work and it was one of the hardest things I have ever done. What if people didn't believe in me? What if they thought the things I was teaching weren't valuable? What if I didn't stand out as a leader? Those were all fears that were constantly pecking at me. But I didn't care! Something deep inside of me knew that it was time to share this information, even at the risk of people not believing in me. But after a few months of teaching, I began to realize that people were reading my words and watching my videos. Massage therapists were taking my knowledge and applying it to their own businesses. They were having success in their own careers!

During this time I was starting to go through some of my own changes in my massage practice. At the beginning of my career, I became an in-network provider for insurance companies - something I truly believe in doing. After five years of being a provider, I was starting to become frustrated and burnt-out financially with one company in particular. Their reimbursement rate hadn't changed in five years and it was low even to begin with. As a seasoned, experienced massage therapist, it was killing me as the years went on to accept this low level of reimbursement and finally I had had enough. It was terrifying, to say the least, to even consider the possibility of no longer accepting this insurance. I knew I was going to be disappointing my clients and saying goodbye to a number of them. I was heartbroken! I lost sleep, felt sick and cried over my decision. But I knew that if I didn't make this change, there was a good chance that this insurance company would be the cause of burn-out and the loss of my career as a massage therapist. I was working myself to death to earn a good living. I had given my power to an insurance company and their low level of pay was killing me. I wrote a heartfelt letter to each of my clients explaining the situation and telling them that in 60 days I would no longer be able to accept their insurance company. The response I received was overwhelming. Most had no idea I wasn't being paid well, many decided to remain a client and just pay out of pocket and others had no choice but to see a new therapist through their insurance. The one thing I realized through it all was that, even though I was terrified of hurting and disappointing my clients, after I made my decision I found a new level of empowerment and strength inside of me that I didn't know existed. The Ann I knew even just a few years before would never have done anything like that. I was too afraid of people thinking badly of me or disappointing them, even at my own expense. This choice showed me that I am growing and evolving each and every year through the challenges and fears that are being placed in front of me. What a blessing!

On top of eliminating this insurance company, I am in the process of hiring my first employee. While I once thought that hiring employees seemed like more hassle than it was worth, I am now realizing the importance of growing my practice. I have felt the effects of taking care of hundreds of people through the years and am recognizing that it's too much for me to handle at this point. As my business continues to grow, it's becoming harder and harder for me to manage everything on my own. I am limited to the number of clients I can see per week and am losing new clients because of it. My schedule is booked out weeks in advance and new clients don't always want to wait that long to get in. Hiring an employee to complement my level of work will not only allow the possibility of taking care of my community with more than 20 massages per week, but it will also allow me to earn an additional stream of income. In addition, it creates a career for a massage therapist in need of a place to work. Hiring my first employee is just another fear I must push through to get to the next level in business.

Although my career and business growth look shiny on the outside, I want to expose the challenges that have faced me through the years. It wouldn't be fair of me to share beauty and not acknowledge the struggle. For light can never be present without dark. It can, at times, overwhelm me to be so needed by people. The constant flow of people in pain - emotional and physical - coming to me needing help is a lot to deal with. I feel guilty at times because I value and appreciate the trust my clients have for me, but on the other hand I can become so drained of energy that I just want to be left alone. In addition, when my personal life presents me with its many challenges, it can be incredibly difficult to stay focused on the needs of others. While some days I just want to stay home and take care of a personal issue, I have to put myself aside and put my clients first. I know that my clients need me and trust me and that is what gets me going in the morning. It's funny, though, because once I am at work, in my massage room, in my space of healing and good energy, I become so focused on my fulfilling work that I often forget about my own problems. Massage therapy fulfills me in a way that nothing else in this world can.

I am still learning to deal with these challenges and am realizing the importance of taking time off for myself and enjoying vacations. I was so focused on building my business in the first five years that I completely forgot about myself. I am finally at a place in my life where I am learning to love myself on the deepest of levels.

What good are we as healers if we are burnt-out and drained all the time? We have to know how to put ourselves first, say no when necessary and create boundaries to keep our space healthy.

These are all things I have learned through the years, personally and professionally. Through my own burn-out and internal struggles, I am finally emerging a new woman, strong and confident. With all of the struggles and challenges owning a business has brought to my life, I have to say that I love this profession for what it has brought to my life, the light and the dark. I have become so much through massage therapy. I sometimes don't even recognize myself any more. I can't believe that I am known for being a source of health in my community, a leader in business ownership and, most importantly, a strong, secure, able woman capable of accomplishing anything she puts her mind to. I am a brand new person because of massage therapy. I have so much beauty, love and joy around me each and every day. I love myself enough now to accept it all with open arms. Massage therapy was my saving grace and I will forever be grateful to her for introducing herself to me. I am a better person because of this profession. I have a purpose now.

There are a number of hidden messages in my story that I want to make sure each and every person picks up on. For my story wouldn't be worth telling if the messages aren't seized. First, take time to figure out who you are as a massage therapist and the vision of your company. This is what your clients will be drawn to when choosing you over the hundreds of other massage therapists in your city. You are more than just a massage therapist; you are a valuable business offering a unique solution to a problem. What makes you so special? Secondly, if you want to be successful, you have to be willing to push your own personal boundaries and face your fears. I was afraid of everything that eventually led to my success. I pushed through each obstacle along the way and found the pot of gold on the other side. Successful people don't run away from what is hard and make excuses. They figure out a way to push forward, even when it's uncomfortable. And let me tell you, it will be incredibly difficult, hard and scary at times. Now that you know that, deal with it, face your fears and go out there and create success! Next, my success came when I took responsibility for myself and my business. When I stopped looking at others to create success for me and saw myself as the employer, not the employee, everything changed for me. If you remain the victim and make excuses, you will never reach the level of success you are capable of. Stand up, take responsibility and take action. You are only as strong as your worst excuse. Remember that! And lastly, things will work out when they are supposed to. Starting a business is hard work and the beginning is typically the hardest. Finding direction and taking action are key aspects of success early on. It may take a year or two for things to really get to a point where you are happy with the amount of massage sessions you are doing. Don't get discouraged because it's not happening right away. If you have the opportunity to create income by working a side job while you build up your business, do it. It will be worth it in the long run not to have to worry about finances in the beginning. Yes, it's hard to work while building a business on the side, but when you look back in 5-10 years, you will be glad you did it. Remember that success is never simple or easy. It takes hard work, especially in the beginning.

Never give up and always believe without a doubt that you can do it. Don't be afraid to spend money on your education. I would never be where I am if I hadn't invested in my business development. I have created hundreds of thousands of dollars because I was willing spend a few thousand dollars on my education. Spending money to learn how to create money is a no-brainer. Don't put all your eggs in one basket when it comes to creating income. Seek out multiple streams of income and secure your future financially. You never know what tomorrow is going to bring. Read self-help books to help remove old programming and seek out professional help if you feel stuck and unable to move forward. We all carry around old programming that we aren't good enough and get stuck at times. You are able to do anything you want to, you just have to get out of your own way to make it happen. I am proof of that.

One last thing I want to touch on is that there is nothing wrong with being an employee. I know we all hear a lot about owning our own businesses and being self-employed, but that is not always for everybody. If you would rather be an employee, by all means go for it. Just please make sure that you are getting paid what you are worth. This trend of paying massage therapists $15-$20 per massage is not OK. You will burn out and resent your work if you aren't making a good living doing it. Massage therapists are incredibly gifted healers who should be compensated appropriately. You are worth so much, so please don't settle for less than you are worth.

Also, just because you are an employee doesn't mean you can't and shouldn't learn how to earn passive income as well. There are opportunities all around us - we just have to seek them out. Look for ways to create multiple streams of income in your life. Trading an hour for a dollar doesn't suit anyone any more. It's time to start thinking outside the box and creating income on different levels.

The future of our profession is so incredibly exciting for me. I look forward to growing my massage practice and continuing to share my knowledge with those in need. I believe each and every one of us has a gift to share with this world. You may not see it at first, or know yourself well enough to expose it, but it will show itself in time. Listen, slow down, go deep inside yourself and you will find it. When the time comes for you to expand yourself in ways other than just massage therapy, go for it. Listen to the ideas that come into your head and expand on them. For all success and inventions started with just a simple thought in someone's mind. Honor the incredible mind that you have and think outside the box. Push through the doors of fear to find your pot of gold waiting on the other side. Where would I be if I hadn't? I'm happy to say that I don't know the answer to that question. I didn't stick around long enough to find out.

Much love and support to you, my fellow massage therapists! You hold a special place in my heart.

ANN ROSS BIO

Ann Ross is a self-employed massage therapist in Seattle, WA where she owns and operates her successful practice. In addition, she educates massage therapists through her website www.MassageMarketingMentor.com, an instrumental resource in helping self-employed massage therapists create successful businesses.

Ann Ross, LMP

www.UrbanHealingArts.com

www.MassageMarketingMentor.com

(425) 501-8712

"Success isn't a result of spontaneous combustion. You must set yourself on fire."

-Arnold H. Glasgow

4

JEFF SAUERS

Before we get started…

OFFICIAL LEGAL DISCLAIMER:

I've never owned or managed a massage therapy center or day spa of any kind. I'm also not a marketing guru, not a motivational speaker, nor have I attended college other than massage therapy school.

To tell you the truth, unlike the majority of our community, I'm really not even "holistic".

I don't walk around barefoot, I can't sit still in the lotus position for more than two minutes without going stir crazy, I *hate* the smell of patchouli, I don't walk around in a state of bliss most of the time, and I don't believe that "the universe will provide" simply because I've "found my passion".

Not that there is anything wrong with the abovementioned. This may be you. Some of the nicest massage therapists I've ever met are this way.

It's just that… *it's not me*. Never was.

To give you even more insight into my sparkling personality, I'm a beer-drinking, meat-eating, rock drummer of more than 20 years. I'm on anti-anxiety medication *(and, yes, I've tried all kinds of natural and homeopathic approaches and nothing has worked yet)*. I use blue language and have been known to put my foot in my mouth occasionally.

As you can see, I definitely DO NOT fit the mold of the typical body worker.

But despite all of my obvious shortcomings, the one thing that I've finally learned to do after many years is to attract massage clients – *a lot of them* – pretty much at will, without spending a dime in advertising, no web site – not even a Google listing – without being able to offer all of the fancy amenities that ritzy day spas have, *and* having to compete with all the other therapists in my area.

I've even had some clients that I've worked on for 15 years. Seriously! *Wait a minute...*

Who the hell am I and why should you pay any attention to me whatsoever? Good question!

My name if Jeff Sauers. I've been a practicing massage therapist in PA from 1993-2009. I've worked for hair salons, day spas, chiropractors, MDs, an osteopath, a chair massage company, a massage franchise, and had my own private and mobile practice.

I've performed massage in almost every environment you can think of, from doctors' offices to business offices, hair salons to elite day spas, convention centers to outside events, hotels to bed & breakfasts, gyms and girls' night out parties, in studio apartments and $1,000,000 homes, in radio stations and in malls... *even in a bus terminal!*

I've sure been around the block in the world of massage.

Even though it's obvious that I'm not the typical massage therapist, there is one universal commonality that I share with every single body worker I've ever met...

"How Do I Get Clients?"

I understand. I've been there myself.

I've been broke when I started out as a massage therapist to the point where I almost gave up, then struck gold and was doing so well that I used to fly to Amsterdam just for long weekends to party my ass off, then went to being broke again to the point where I had to sell off my IRA accounts and take side jobs bartending just to make ends meet, to finally balancing being a therapist *and* making good money.

Before I share some client-attracting secrets I've learned throughout the years, I want to give you a little more of my background. I think it's important that you get to know me and my story first so that you'll really be able to understand and see that if *I'm* able to be a successful massage therapist – even though I'm the opposite of the stereotypical therapist – *then anyone can.*

In 1993 I was a 23-year-old budding rock drummer with stars in his eyes and no additional training or skills other than a high school diploma. Didn't need any. I mean, stardom was just around the corner. You don't need a college degree to be on MTV *(I wanted to be free from structured education, anyway.*

However, I *was* sick and tired of working at low-paying jobs during the day. That got old quick.

One day as I was waiting for the train to take me home after working yet another day of mind-numbingly boring work, I got into a conversation with this girl. It turns out that she was going to school for massage therapy.

I was very interested in hearing more about it. I've been receiving chiropractic adjustments most of my life, so I thought that massage therapy would be a great career for me. It's not 9-5, it pays well, it's a growing field, I'm a people-person, it's low stress – *this is the perfect career for me!*

So I enrolled at a massage school in center city Philadelphia. I was able to work during the days and go to school at nights and weekends.

As graduation time came closer, students started asking how they should go about finding employment or get their own practice off the ground. The only advice given to us was: "*Send cover letters to day spas and chiropractic offices. Print up business cards and brochures to hand out. Tell people about your new practice.*" (Sound familiar already?)

As a good student – and not knowing any better – that's exactly what I did. I also noticed that this was exactly how every other massage practitioner was marketing themselves. And they should know. I mean, they're the experts, right?

I had a professional-looking cover letter printed that described my education as well as going into detail about what a good, eager, hard-working person I was. I mailed it out to every day spa, hair salon and chiropractic office in the phone book without a single response.

I also printed up business cards and a massage brochure for my fledgling mobile practice. Just like the cover letters, not one person called.

After a few months, panic started to set in. Was going to massage therapy school a complete waste of time?

This was when I learned the first of many valuable lessons, although I didn't apply them right away:

Massage therapy schools and organizations are very good at teaching you various massage techniques, contraindications, anatomy... but they're not experts on marketing.

Just because they know how to teach massage, that doesn't mean they automatically know the best marketing techniques. And I'm saying this with all due respect to them.

Here's an analogy that I like to use: just because you know how to drive a car doesn't automatically make you an auto mechanic, does it? Of course not. They are two *completely* different skills. Just because you love listening to music doesn't automatically make you a musician.

To make a long story short, I eventually found some work through sheer hard work and persistence. Admittedly, some of the work that I've received came simply because I was in the right place at the right time. Chalk it up to luck, I guess. *(One time I was hired because a receptionist at a chiropractor's office thought I was cute!)*

Then in 1996 I started working for an MD who had a large rehabilitation section and plenty of patients. Through a combination of work from the MD, a chiropractor I started working for part-time, plus my own mobile practice on the side, I was working steadily six days a week. I didn't think it would end.

Then in 2002, the rehab section shut down. Within a month, I went from having six or seven (or more) hour-long sessions a day to having only two or three a week. This is no way to pay the bills.

It was a sickening feeling to have to start from the bottom after being a successful massage practitioner for almost 10 years. I knew I had a lot to offer, but I also knew that letting someone else dictate to me what I was worth and being dependent upon someone else for my income wasn't the answer. I looked myself in the mirror and decided that I will never again rely on someone else for my income.

In the meantime, I was also taking various massage marketing seminars, bought and studied all the books, cassettes and CDs, purchased home study courses, visited websites and subscribed to free online newsletters from all the massage marketing "experts" out there. To my shock, I soon discovered that most of the marketing information I was receiving from our community wasn't working.

I followed their advice to the letter with very little, if any, real results. Most of the information was either flat out wrong, wasn't detailed enough or didn't equip practitioners with reliable templates to follow that actually worked and systemized the marketing process from beginning to end.

At this time I was still working for a chiropractor part-time. Luckily, I was able to use the massage room any time I pleased. I was allowed to turn that into my own business if I wanted.

So I started looking outside the massage world for solid marketing strategies that consistently and effectively produced results. After lots of research and testing other marketing methods that were vastly different from what I'd been taught in massage school, I actually started seeing results… *and fast*!

These are the types of results I was getting:

The first idea I decided to test was mailing a very personal and fun-to-read letter to about 80 of the chiropractor's patients about a new massage session I was offering. And this letter was *not* your typical *"50% off deep tissue massage"* that you see everywhere. It was more of a personal letter than a sales letter.

And it worked! We got about 15 new massage appointments from this one letter alone. That's about a 20% response rate.

I used this same personal approach for generating referrals. Not only did it work, but to my surprise, our patients didn't realize that I was looking for referrals.

Then I used this same formula to promote gift certificates during the holiday season. I sold dozens of them with almost no effort at all.

Next, I designed a simple flyer for our counter display sign and, believe it or not, it sold seven gift certificates in just the first three hours of being on our counter, not including the additional sales it generated within the next couple of weeks.

To make a long story short, my schedule was suddenly full within a few weeks. And the best part is that this was done without a website, without spending money on expensive advertising, no software I had to invest in, and without resembling every other massage therapist in my area.

In fact, clients actually started looking forward to my "junk" mail and asking me when I was going to send them something again.

So I started writing down what I've been applying and in January 2008, I released my first marketing course for massage therapists. It was so much fun showing other therapists from around the world how to generate clients.

But the one thing that I noticed when I was starting out, and I still hear it when talking with both new and experienced massage therapists today, is how unbelievably difficult it is to either find steady employment and/or to know the secrets to consistently generate massage clients.

This was true when I first graduated massage school, and it's still true to this day.

So now I'm going to share with you six discoveries that really helped me have a successful massage practice quickly and affordably. There are actually more than six, but these are the ones that helped turn everything around for me.

The first thing I realized when I decided to take my career into my own hands is that finding your passion isn't enough. Don't get me wrong – I firmly *do* believe that finding your calling is vitally important to your overall happiness. If you believe that doing bodywork really, really is your life's calling – *good for you!* Most people in life don't even search for it.

I've never met a group of people who truly believed with every cell in their bodies that they found their calling more than massage therapists.

And most of them are also broke. Ironic, isn't it? They found their calling, but the universe isn't providing. Something's wrong here.

The way many massage practitioners believe their business should grow is very similar to the old baseball park cliché: *"If we build it, they will come."* Meaning: *"I am a good, well-intentioned massage therapist. The universe will provide."*

I, too, am a believer in sending out positive energy and well-intentioned thoughts, but I also believe *"God helps those who help themselves."*

Even the most respected experts in the field of personal growth such as Dr Wayne Dyer, Napoleon Hill and Deepak Chopra will say that you must take action on your thoughts.

However, simply being "good" or "well-intentioned" isn't nearly enough. I mean, every massage practitioner is "good" and "well-intentioned" or else we wouldn't be in this business.

The interesting thing I found was that all of the massage practitioners I've come in contact with over the years who held this belief were scraping for work. *(Maybe the universe is trying to send them a lesson instead.)*

Many practitioners also believe that just because you've satisfied a client, that client will go out of their way to tell others about you.

Sometimes that happens. But more often than not, they just go on with their lives. People are busy. Everyone has a million things to do that day.

Why should they go out of their way to talk about you to other people? What are you offering them in return? Why should they promote you over any business they come in contact with that day?

Think about it. All of us are extremely busy. Do you always go out of your way to talk about a particular restaurant or bookstore or product or service provider of any kind just because you had a good experience with them? Rarely.

Just assuming that people will go home and talk about how wonderful their experience was with you to everyone they know is strictly ego-driven. Unfortunately, I've talked to many massage practitioners over the years who think that.

The second thing I've noticed that really helps attract and keep clients is to communicate in a conversational tone. I recently coined this term *Conversational Marketing*. *Conversational Marketing* is the art and skill of wording what you have to offer in ways that attract people's attention, generate their interest and lead them to further action. I firmly believe that if you master the skill of *Conversational Marketing*, you will hold in your hands the key to generating clients and prospects at will and have the practice of your dreams.

If there is ONE THING that I attribute my success to, more than any other, it is the ability to craft an effective sales message that people can easily relate to.

This skill will be used in your sales letters, flyers, advertising, brochures, business cards, website, face-to-face – anything that applies to promoting yourself and your practice.

Even if you're a specialist or know every massage technique known to man...

What good will they be if you can't effectively communicate to people what you can do for them and – even more important – get your phone ringing for appointments?

Let me ask you if you've ever experienced this...

Have you ever been to a psychic, tarot card reader, or palm reader – whether that person was legitimate or a real good fake – and that person said something that stopped you dead in your tracks and you thought to yourself: *"How the hell did he/she know that?"*

If you've ever experienced this, time seemed to stand still for a moment, didn't it? It's happened to me a few times and it freaked me out. *"Is this person for real? Or is he/she a very good fake?"*

Maybe it didn't come from a psychic. It could've come from a religious speaker, salesperson, mentalist, politician – anybody. You were *instantly* tuned into what this person has to say next, weren't you?

Nobody had to convince you to pay attention to this person. *They instantly got your attention!*

Why did you experience this? It's because that person communicated something to you in a way that spoke to your core. It resonated something inside of you.

Let me describe a scenario for you. Let's say you're having lunch with a real close friend. During lunch, your friend starts complaining about headaches she always gets.

Do you think she would describe her symptoms this way:

"I believe my C1 and C2 vertebrae aren't in proper alignment. Also, the muscle fibers in my cervical area are causing trigger points that are referring to my temporal region."

Hell no! She would probably describe her headaches this way...

"Mary, this damn headache has been killing me for two days! It feels like someone is stabbing my eyeball. I can't get any work done and my boss is going to be pissed. It got so bad I snapped at the poor waiter at the restaurant last night. I don't know what else to do to make it go away."

Now would you – as a massage therapist – say to her:

"Well, Karen, the reason why you're experiencing severe headaches is probably because of trigger points firing from your cervical area into your temporal region that's causing a high amount of neurological activity. Myofascial release removes unwanted toxins that impede healing and brings harmony to your mind, body, and spirit, and gives you a better overall sense of well being."

Of course you wouldn't! I think your friend Karen would stab *YOU* in the eye if you worded it that way.

However, notice that *ALL* marketing material for therapists to give to others is worded the same way. Every one of them. Without exception.

Now if you wouldn't talk to a friend using confusing, boring gibberish that they can't relate to, then don't use it for clients and prospects. When I started using empathy in the way I communicated with my clients – whether I was using letters, postcards, flyers, business cards, face-to-face, whatever – I noticed my response rates skyrocket. I mean, it was freaky. Clients started telling me things like: *"How did you know that's exactly how I'm feeling?"*

The third component that I started noticing is that this is a relationship business, not a transactional business. One thing that I've discovered over the years is that clients really don't have an interest in experiencing all of the techniques I've learned. Most of them wanted basically the same type of massage.

Then why did I have clients that were loyal to me for 10 years or more when I was doing the same type of massage over and over? The reason is because of the relationship we developed with each other over the years.

You see, clients want to know you as a person – not as a massage therapist. Don't mistake the point. Your actual massage skills are only going to keep them coming back to you for so long. But the more they feel connected to you, the longer they stay. I did the opposite of what others in our community do.

For example, I talk to my clients. I don't work in silence unless I get the vibe that they want it quiet. And I definitely don't shush them. I've seen therapists do this. They say: *"Shhh. Please don't talk. This is your time."* Oh *puh-lease!* Talking is the best way to develop rapport with each other. They truly want to know about you and your life. Seriously – they do!

When my clients came into the massage room, we continued the conversation that we had when we last saw each other. This is what kept them coming back month after month. They often said things like: *"What's new, Jeff? How's your two fat cats? Did you and your wife conceive yet? Are you still in your band? Planning a trip to Amsterdam any time soon? What did you think of the Eagles game last Sunday?"*

So don't be all "professional" and work in silence. Don't be afraid to open up to your clients. They LOVE it and want to hear more. I'm not talking about revealing family secrets, just talk to them like you do your close friends. This is what bonds them to you and keeps them coming back.

The fourth discovery I've made is not to look like everyone else. This is a crucial marketing mistake that practically every massage practitioner makes. This mistake is made from independent practitioners as well as owners and managers of large day spas.

Have you ever noticed that practically every massage practitioner's marketing material looks identical to everyone else's?

It's called Traditional Marketing and it simply doesn't work.

What I'm talking about is the typical business card/brochure format that has the practitioner's name, a cute logo in the corner, a list of their techniques which most people don't understand, a phone number, and the words *"by appointment only"*.

Unfortunately, probably 99% of massage practitioners make the mistake of what I call *"sameness"*. Their marketing material is the same as every other massage practitioner, day spa, etc.

Here's a fun and eye-opening experiment to do:

Take a look at every massage advertising piece you can find, including yours, whether it's a Yellow Pages ad, business cards and brochures, free health newsletters in doctor's offices waiting rooms, flyers, classified ads, websites – anything, and notice what they all have in common.

You'll quickly see they are all basically the same.

The typical massage practitioner's business cards or brochures usually resemble something like this:

Karen Jones, LMT

Swedish, Reflexology, Sports Massage, Seated Chair, Reiki.

AMTA Member

By appointment only.

Call...

Most massage practitioners just go with the flow and print the same information that their peers wrote for their own business cards, brochures or flyers.

They copy the copycats who copied the copycats who copied the copycats. I call it the *"Where's Waldo"* syndrome.

We've all seen the popular Where's Waldo children's books. You have to search very carefully in a page filled with dozens and dozens of other red and white striped people to find Waldo.

So when you're putting together your marketing material, ask yourself:

"Does mine stand out from all the rest or does it blend in with every other massage practitioner's advertising material?"

Unfortunately, most massage practitioners and day spas have one common problem: Everybody is saying the same thing. Everyone has the same message.

And what's worse – *nobody understands it!*

Now, look at it through the eyes of a potential client and seriously ask yourself this question that you absolutely MUST have an answer to:

"Why should someone choose me over any other massage practitioner in my area?"

Listing all your education and associations is called "feature dumping".

It only mentions what you're offering, but says absolutely nothing about the benefits a person will have with their experience with you.

And even if people do know what a few of these terms mean, why should they choose you over any other practitioner who is offering the same massage modalities?

Are you offering anything different that sets you apart from your competition?

Are you specializing in a particular problem/technique/group of people? Are you using terms and phrases that the average person understands?

The reality is people make buying decisions out of emotion, not out of logic or seeing a grocery list of massage modalities that they don't understand.

The fifth component that kept clients booking regularly is by keeping constant contact with them. Many therapists have clients who booked regularly and then all of a sudden disappear.

Day spas and practitioners alike assume that clients will automatically think of them when they want another massage.

They just sit back and wait for the phone to ring. They'll call when they need a massage again... *or will they?*

The key is to always let them know you're still there.

Many therapists are unaware of the power and importance of building a solid relationship with their clients and always keeping in contact with them, no matter how much you believe that you have them as a client for life and you don't need to do anything extra to keep in touch.

Here are some statistics from a well-known marketing survey about why businesses lose customers:

- 1% die;

- 3% move;

- 5% switch to a friend or family member's recommendation

- 9% find a better product or service;

- 14% are dissatisfied with the product or service.

The fact is that all of these reasons added up together equal only 32%. What about the other 68%?

A full 68% switched to a different product or service provider simply because of indifference.

They didn't feel important or have a real reason to stay loyal. There was nothing new the business was offering for their clients.

For example, there were no:

- new products;

- new services;

- discounts;

- postcards;

- sales letters;

- newsletters;

- referral programs;

- recognitions;

- thank you cards;

- birthday cards.

The client simply feels that the store/service provider doesn't care whether or not they receive their business.

The customer doesn't feel appreciated or feel that their business matters. You need to keep in constant contact with them at least 8-12 times a year.

You need to be proactive at staying at the front of their minds when it comes to getting a massage.

Don't leave it up to hoping or assuming they'll always remember you and call you. *They won't!*

Now if you're thinking at this point: *"This all sounds great, Jeff, but how do I get clients in the first place?"*

Well, I didn't give you the sixth discovery that jumpstarted my private practice.

The No 1 method that brought new clients into my practice was by having local service-oriented businesses endorse me to their clients/customers. I asked them if they would be so kind as to hand out to their clients a "thank you" letter that appeared as if it were written by the business owner that goes out to their database thanking them for being such a great client/customer. Their database also gets a free gift certificate for a 10-15-minute massage by me.

This is how you do this...

For example, a hair stylist who is a client of yours can mail or hand out a letter that's written by *"them"* but is actually written by you offering their clients a free 10-15-minute massage with you as a thank you for being such loyal customers.

The letter goes on to say how wonderful your massage sessions are, how well you treat the hair stylist, how long you've known each other, etc.

This works for many reasons.

Her clients already trust her. They already have a good relationship with each other.

Those clients are much more likely to believe what that hair stylist says about your practice than what you say about your practice.

There Is *Instant* Credibility And Believability.

Why would a business personally endorse someone who wasn't reputable, reliable and gave great service?

They wouldn't. It would only hurt *their* business and credibility.

There are three powerful reasons why this benefits everybody:

1) The business owner looks good to their customers by appearing as if they purchased the free 10-15-minute massage. It shows good will to their customers. In addition,

the business owner isn't even writing it. You are. They simply look the letter over and approve it. There is absolutely no extra work for them to do.

2) Their customers are getting a free gift with absolutely no strings attached as a thank you for being such good customers. This helps strengthen the bond between the business and their customers.

3) You benefit by acquiring new prospects that you can now nurture into lifetime clients. Also, you'll have new names and addresses to add to your mailing list to continually market to and always stay at the top of their minds when they think about massage.

That's the reason why this is the most perfect system to start a massage practice from scratch.

It is without question the best system for stimulating a constant stream of clients, even if you're fresh out of massage school.

Keep this in mind...

- What you say about you may or may not be true.

- What someone else says about you is more likely to be true.

- If two or more people say good things about you, then it's probably true.

- If someone else *prints* something good about you, then it's definitely true!

Let me give you a scenario. Let's say that you're Joe Schmo who's thinking of getting a massage. However, you don't know who to call. Every massage therapist in the Yellow Pages or on Google resembles each other.

Then you get a personalized letter in the mail from your doctor endorsing a massage therapist along with a gift certificate for a free massage sample.

Who would you be more inclined to call – someone who you randomly found online or someone your own doctor is raving about? The therapist that your very own doctor is personally endorsing, of course! It's a no-brainer.

This is what kick-started my private practice. And the best thing about it is that it costs no money to do. Let me give you a real life example:

The very first person that I tried this out with was a long-time client of mine who owns a dog grooming business. She handed out 25 gift certificates for a free 15-minute massage with me to her best clients.

Seven of them got redeemed and four of the seven became regular clients. And it didn't cost either one of us a penny. That's a 28% response rate!

And remember – four of them became regular clients. Let's assume that those four only got a massage from me just three times a year. Let's also assume that I charge $60 an hour. That's $720 (not including tip) from these four clients alone. And that doesn't include any testimonials I'll get, future bookings, referrals, gift certificate purchases – I mean, it doesn't stop with just one appointment.

Imagine if you had a nail technician, hair stylist, travel agent, health food store owner, and a chiropractor handing out a thank you letter along with a gift certificate for a free massage sample from you to their clients/customers. And let's assume that only 10 of them got redeemed. Out of those 10, four of them booked only two-hour massage sessions with you during their lifetime *(these are very conservative numbers if you're still skeptical at this point)*. And let's say that you charged $60 an hour. That's still a $480 profit!

Again, these are very conservative numbers. Now let's also assume that you kept this process going week after week. You'll be receiving four regular clients a week for the rest of your career.

I know massage therapists who have been in practice for literally decades who would kill to have this kind of success rate. They just sit at home waiting for their phone to ring. They are doing absolutely NOTHING proactive to stimulate their practice.

So to sum up this chapter, if you...

1) Understand that finding your passion and being at one with the universe isn't enough to attract massage clients

2) Communicate with people in a conversational tone that they can understand and relate to

3) Realize that this is a relationship business, not a transactional one

4) Don't look like every other therapist out there

5) Keep regular contact with them

6) Have other people promote you to give you instant credibility

...you're gonna do just fine! And if you ever have any questions, please feel free to contact me anytime. I can be reached at info@ultimatemassagesuccess.com.

Thanks!

JEFF SAUERS BIO

Jeff Sauers has been a well respected massage therapist and relaxation expert for 16 years, specializing in teaching fun, outside-the-box techniques that get clients inside your practice. He is the proprietor of UltimateMassageSuccess.com, teaching how to get local businesses promoting your massage practice, as well as HybridMassageTherapyPractice.com, a site that teaches how any massage therapist can work in any day spa or doctor's office they please even if you're just out of massage school. He exposes the truth of how easy it really is.

www.UltimateMassageSuccess.com

www.HybridMassgeTherapyPractice.com

www.Twitter.com/Massage_Success

www.UltimateMassageSuccess.Blogspot.com

www.Facebook.com/UltimateMassageSuccess

The greatness of a community is most accurately measured by the compassionate actions of its members, ... a heart of grace and a soul generated by love.

- Coretta Scott King

5

KARLA LINDEN

I joke around a lot that there wasn't a table or booth for massage therapy in my High School Career Fair. Of course, that was in the late 1970s. Things have certainly changed now. Some days I can call back first memories of rubbing my grandmother's feet or massaging her scalp – and I guess I was about three or four when I began as a "natural" massage therapist. I've always loved the skin, learning about anatomy and physiology, and have enjoyed developing palpation skills. Over the many years I've been in practice, I've worked with movie stars, CEOs of international companies, more than 100 touring dance and music groups, as varied as KISS, John Denver and Kurt Cobain, Kevin Klein and Brad Pitt, but the biggest honor of my life was to be in service to Mrs. Martin Luther King Jr. (Coretta Scott King) as her massage therapist for more than four years.

To
Karla

With my love and
deepest Appreciation for
the loving services which
you have performed for
me and for all of
the things you do to
help keep ~~so~~ many
People healthy. . . .

Xmas 1992   Coretta Scott King

Thank you note from Coretta Scott King

Looking back now, many things drew me to massage therapy, but I became a client when I was 19. I was working in a very stressful job sitting in front of a computer for the company that was the licensing agent for Cabbage Patch Kids in Atlanta, Georgia. I had this pain in the middle of my back – right where I could not reach – and a co-worker suggested that I get a massage. I really did not know where to begin to find a massage therapist, so I called a classified ad in Creative Loafing – Atlanta's free weekly paper. I remember the first time I went – I was so nervous – and the entire question of whether I should leave my undies on or take them off was a big issue! So I began to get regular massage from a wonderful therapist, Kathleen Spisak Ernst, who has since passed away. The more massage I received, the more I thought "Wow, I would like to do this" and "I wonder if I COULD do this?" and three years later I took the plunge. I remember after my third massage or so, driving home in the car and really FEELING my feet – for the first time ever having that awareness. And another time, after a fourth or fifth massage, getting undressed to take a shower. As I walked through the bathroom, I caught a glimpse of myself naked in the mirror, and realized it was the first time I had looked at myself naked and not been hypercritical or self-loathing – I felt accepting. This was a HUGE gift and one that I wanted to share with others. However, it was a big dilemma to consider giving up a regular paycheck and jumping off the cliff of self-employment. I have to say, looking back, that it was the best choice I ever made, and a challenge that I'm glad I faced at the youngish age of 22.

There are far too many things to list out about this profession that I love, that I've given my life to. I love that every morning when I wake up, I am in awe that this is my work – and I get to BE with people and get paid for it! I'm grateful that I'm in a lovely environment, surrounded by art and beautiful furniture, and that I get to BE with beloved clients all day long. My company name is Masterpiece Medical Massage – named that because I feel and believe that the human body is God's greatest masterpiece. I also love that doing this work is instant gratification – I can see with eyes and feel with my hands the benefits that unfold right underneath my nose! I am so grateful that the immediate relief people get from the hour on the table is translated through their smiling eyes when they hug me "good-bye". It makes me happy to receive massage therapy, too, because I learn so much from receiving, a deepening of my own relationship with my body, and a greater and greater understanding of the miracle we all are.

I also love that we each can be our full self-expression, whatever that looks like, and in doing so help our clients see that they can safely be fully self-expressed. That in accepting ourselves, and modeling self-acceptance, it can't help but bubble over and bless each person we come in contact with.

I feel that I'm an "expert" or "contributor" in the field of massage therapy because over the past 24 years I've had the constant pursuit of improving my skills, developing different niches, and trying all the different things that I could dream of. And that I've created opportunities and embraced changes in this field as time has passed. For instance, when I began practicing, there was only one massage school in Georgia, and no state licensure. I took the National Boards in 1994 – not because they were required in the state I was in, but because I wanted to have as many credentials and demonstrate my commitment to excellence in this field. Another thing that I've always strived to do is to study with the best teachers I could find – from Deane Juhan (author of Job's Body), Thea Elijah, Lic. Acupuncturist, Whitfield Reaves, Lic. Acupuncturist, Thomas Meyers (former head of the Rolf Institute anatomy department, author of Anatomy Trains), Carole Osborn-Sheets, LMT, Jeanne Aland, NMT, LMT, Dr Rosita Arvigo, ND, and many others.

I did "the math" once and it occurred to me that I have done more than 10,000 massages in my career, and have probably received at least 500. I think that adds to mastery and to a quality of touch and understanding that cannot be taught in any other way except practice and experience. I'm grateful that at 47 I'm now an "old hand" in this business, in the most literal way.

I've had many personal and professional challenges over the years. Twenty-five years ago, announcing that I was a massage therapist at a cocktail party or out in public was a bit risky, and might raise eyebrows, or get me into a conversation where I was referred to as a "masseuse". I still (rarely) deal with male inquiries over the phone that help me to sharpen my intuition and clarity about the fact that I do strictly therapeutic work. I wish and hope and pray that our profession gets more accepted and regarded – I've seen that happen over the years, and want more of it for us all. When I began, there was no state licensure in Georgia, and I met the Secretary of State personally to ask for it. Fortunately, this has changed, and Georgia now has licensure. One of my biggest personal obstacles was thinking that I had to do it "all by myself", and making the shift from being a sole practitioner to having a larger practice (and doing some management as well as hands-on treatments). Another series of obstacles was to evaluate and re-evaluate my business model, and be courageous enough to make shifts and changes in it. I've had about every type of practice I could dream of – working out of my home, working in a professional office of my own in a medical building, doing only house calls (to very wealthy clients who had their own massage tables), working backstage at concert venues and on movie sets, having a practice that focused on pregnant women, and in mid-2008, at the age of 45, I moved across the country to New Mexico, where I did not know anyone, and re-invented my practice all over again. It has been exhilarating.

One of the things that heavily contributed to overcoming those obstacles was moving to a new city (Albuquerque, NM), and enrolling in a Masters' program at the Southwest Acupuncture College. When I began school, I had the old mindset that I would be a lone wolf practitioner, but I started to see the possibility that I could have a group practice and if I did more management, it would be a better, more workable solution. This was a big stretch for me.

I am grateful for every opportunity that has allowed me to get out of a rut, re-create myself, and rise up higher. Many times, the struggles I thought were insurmountable were there for a very good growth reason, and I bless them all.

One belief I had to change to see outside results in my life was the fear of letting go of a regular paycheck and becoming self-employed, that working in private practice could be a possibility for me. A book that really had a big impact on me on many levels was Joy's Way by Dr Brugh Joy, which sits on a shelf in my treatment room. I also had a major belief-system shift when I attended The

Forum in the early 1980s – coming out of those two weekends and evening was the opening that I COULD do this work as my living, and I allowed myself to take the risk and take the plunge. I also had to overcome the belief that I had to do everything myself. I remember declaring to an old boyfriend, in my first year of practice, that I would make $100K doing massage – he was really skeptical!

Although I sincerely enjoy and celebrate the work I do, I have had a life-long struggle with depression, and there are days when I don't want to get out of bed, answer the phone, or go into the office – but once I get motivated and make it happen, I'm always glad. Learning to ask for another appointment before the client leaves my office was a big fear to overcome, and advice I would give to any massage therapist, new or old, is REBOOK – it is the secret to success! Do whatever it takes – role-play, practice, get a coach, until it is "second nature" to you.

Some key pieces of advice that I would give massage therapists just starting out are:

- Get as much additional specific training as you can, and find a niche to work in – specialize!

- Don't be afraid to refer clients to other therapists, and ask for referrals!

- Don't under-price your valuable services – think very hard before you consider giving discounts. I do not give any discounts in my business model – I position myself as the best, and charge accordingly.

- Get regular bodywork – massage, chiropractic, acupuncture. I learn so much when I'm "on the table" and seek out a variety of different bodywork styles. I also make it a priority to get massage and other bodywork from the best in the business – whenever a teacher is coming through town, I try to get an appointment.

- Invest in yourself and your practice – get as much quality continuing education as you can, buy and maintain the best equipment that is available, use the highest quality products (lubricant, liniments, linen) – clients KNOW the difference. I have used the Body Support System BodyCushion for almost 18 years now – and clients love it – along with a TDP heat lamp, in addition to all the other things I do. Add value, and know that you are worth it, your clients are worth it, and they will pay you for it.

• Key pieces of advice I would give massage therapists feeling mental, emotional or physical burn-out include:

• Pace yourself – set a boundary for the number of treatments you can do per day/per week, and stick with it.

• Have written policies for your clients and stick with those too – be consistent with your no-show policy and new client intake forms.

• Key pieces of information I would give massage therapists looking to expand their businesses come from my own personal experience:

• Once again, specialize! Find a niche and become the region's expert on it. Go deep in one or two areas – it makes it easier to gain expertise, and easier to succinctly talk about it. Become the "go to" person for endometriosis or eczema – and clients will flock to you.

• Learn whatever marketing skills you can, that feel "right" to you, and commit to doing something to build your practice every day. One of the basic books that helped me tremendously as I began was Guerrilla Marketing, by Jay Conrad Levinson, and I would highly recommend it. Also Blue Poppy Press's Points for Profit, which is geared towards acupuncturists, but has a lot of good information that is directly applicable to a massage practice. Cherie Sohnen-Moe has some wonderful books and is a great resource, and, of course, Meagan Holub's excellent book is a must-read for a new therapist. I got so much out of Meagan's first book, which proves that even "old dogs" can learn something new.

In fact, have the attitude that every day you will learn something new to improve yourself and your practice – and commit to being a life-long learner. These days, learning about how to use social media and the internet isn't optional. You have to do whatever it takes to acquire this skill – or find a trustworthy person to do it for you. My practice regularly gets 8–10 inquiries a week from our web presence.

This thing we do is not work. It is JOY. It is contribution. It is BLISS. That old saying "work like you don't need the money" can be applied 10-fold in the area of massage therapy. Get regular bodywork, develop a business model that works for you and stick with it, ask for referrals, be flexible in your scheduling, and always, always, ALWAYS have FUN. Figure out what your gifting areas are and use them in every way you can. Don't be afraid to be the wonderful individual YOU. For example, my office is decorated with 1950s mid-century modern furniture along with the Asian theme I love. I collect this furniture, and it is a total joy to be in an environment that is beautiful, professional, yet fun. I'm also a tattoo enthusiast and I'm heavily tattooed. Many of my clients also have tattoos, many do not, but I don't hide myself and who I am. Instead, I work it. I admit that I might not be everybody's cup of tea, yet in this world, who is? I'm grateful that I attract in the ideal client, and gently release those who might be better served elsewhere.

Another piece of advice to MTs starting out: begin developing your contact list as soon as possible. Sit down and think about who you know – and who they know. Ask for help. Several times I asked a client to write a personal letter of recommendation (back before email!) and also to provide me with a copy of their subdivision directory, sorority list, church or country club directory, then I paid to copy and mail the letter. I got many clients from this method, over and over. A "warm" sincere introduction beats a cold call any day of the week.

When I was in elementary school I thought I would grow up to be a librarian or an archaeologist. The idea of growing up to be a massage therapist was not even remotely a possibility. I'm astonished at least once per day when I look down at the person who trusted me to be of service to them, and think to myself: "I get PAID for this!" What a fabulous career, and what a place of humble service. As I exhale I think, over again: "Thank you, thank you, thank you."

One thing I say to clients as well is that in this lifetime, for some reason, I chose not to have children – and at 47 I think that is a "done deal". However, I love being of service to women working on fertility challenges, pregnant women, and women in the post-natal period. I think on some level, in this lifetime, I've taken on being motherly to many, as opposed to a mother to just one or two. This suits my personality and the career I've chosen.

KARLA LINDEN BIO

Karla Linden, LMT, NMT has integrated her passion for bodywork and extensive education, including an internship in China and studying with Dr. Rosita Arvigo, with successful marketing skills to create Masterpiece Medical Massage, a thriving practice in Albuquerque, New Mexico.

Karla Linden, LMT, NMT

Masterpiece Massage Therapy

Albuquerque, New Mexico

(505) 340-9454

www.KarlaLinden.com

www.MasterpieceMassage.com

www.CarCrashMassage.com

"When the world says, "Give up,"Hope
whispers, "Try it one more time."
- Author Unknown

6

SHAUNA FLAGG

I have always had a flair for leadership and making people laugh. I grew up in the beautiful seacoast town of Wells, Maine, with my parents and am the oldest of four siblings. I have always felt more mature in my thought process than my peers when it came to the way life ebbed and flowed. I lost interest in school but still kept up with outside activities and tried my best to find out what I really wanted in life - thinking back on this now, I should have just had fun but I couldn't get my mind to stop working and wondering what life would bring instead of just living in the moment. I am a planner and constantly over-analyzing if I should have done something differently. I have had my whole life planned subconsciously and didn't even know it and it was all from me, not any outside influence. I will touch on that later.

After graduating high school I was accepted to two colleges in the state but didn't think they were the place for me, so I went to a massage school open house - needless to say, my parents were not thrilled! But by the end of the tour, when my mom was receiving a seated chair massage (nice marketing technique), she looked at me and said: "You have to do this." Little did my mom know that going to a college and living that life probably would have been the end of my college career because I just didn't know what direction I wanted to go in and I probably would have flunked out for lack of interest. I love education and can't get enough of it but I have to have passion and purpose to do it. I have always done what I enjoy in life and can't see how people do what they dislike - it would drive me crazy! I had to be passionate and I convinced my parents (which I did truly believe myself) that once I knew what I wanted to do, I would go back to college and this would help pay for it. But it was too late - I loved massage and loved massage school. I had to grow up fast because I was one of the youngest students to be accepted at my massage school at that time and, as everyone knows, you learn a lot about yourself and who you really are by learning about touch.

My favorite part of massage therapy is injury work and intuition. Let me explain. I don't always know exactly how I am going to help someone fully until I start working on them. The client can tell me where it hurts and what they did that started the pain process, but it's my hands that tell me what to do. If I use my intuition and let my hands feel/learn the area of discomfort, then I can help the client. I actually get a little giddy when someone comes in with something I know I can help relieve. That is when I feel I have done my job. Many clients tell me: "It's like you know exactly where to go." I correct them and say no, but my hands do. I can't explain how I know - I just do, and that thrills me that I can do that. I love to help people so I work with a lot of chiropractors, doctors, physical therapists, personal trainers and nutritionists.

My belief system was a little bit twisted in the beginning and I do think that where you start in your massage career is very important. If you don't know where you want to be, then try everything out. Do the spa business, chiropractor/medical office, and try on your own in a small space. See what you are made of and what makes you passionate about this business. This will help you see what best suits you in what you want to do. Do you want to work for someone or do you want to do it on your own? If you want to do it on your own, first work for the kind of business you want and learn as much as possible. My first job was a resort area-type job. It was a local massage clinic but it was high-volume appointments. If I worked a shift, I was guaranteed five appointments. I always worked four to five shifts a week extra and did many outcalls ... I did on average 20-30 appointments a week. I would train the new therapists on the specific technique we were required to use and did a lot of the bookings, money exchange and answering of phones. This was exhausting but let me know that I had stamina to do it. I prefer doing three to four appointments a day, three to four days a week, but the more years of experience, it seems the busier you will get. I was a robot for those first three to four years and found no satisfaction in that kind of work, plus I was told I had to do a specific sequence - no exceptions. If you start to hate what you are doing and feel burnt-out, then re-evaluate the place you are working. It might be the place, not you, that is giving you this feeling.

After leaving that resort spa, I went to a well-known local clinic and was busy right from the start. I still didn't realize that I could do whatever I wanted and not the set sequence that was expected previously. I was still learning how the business worked and knew that if I could do the high energy work at the resort spa, I could do it on my own much easier. I did all the rebooking, answered phone calls, took money, called clients ... I was my own boss, apart from the owner, and I had my own room. We did a 50% split and she supplied everything. It turned out to be a great deal for both of us and I stayed at the clinic for four years, but then again the voice in my head kept saying: what else do you want for your life? I questioned how long I could do massage. So I decided to go back to school. At that time I was 25 and really was an all-or-nothing type of person then. I sent a letter to all of my clients letting them know when I was leaving and telling them that if they would like house visits, I was willing to do that for the same price as coming to the clinic. Even though I was professional and upfront with the owner, there still was some animosity, which is expected but it definitely put a bad note on our relationship. I couldn't do the volume and go to school full-time and I knew I needed to make the $600-$800 a week I was making at the clinic. I wanted a bachelor's degree to fall back on if ever I decided to stop doing massage therapy. I attended New Hampshire Technical College, concentrated in science classes and got a degree in liberal arts to start myself out - all while doing house calls.

Then I moved back to the seacoast and was deciding to attend the local university to get a degree in molecular biology and biochemistry. As I went through the process, I started a small practice in a local athletic club by renting a room for $300 a month. At the same time, I was still traveling to the city I moved from once or twice a week to accommodate the house call clients, and got a job at the university health services doing massage on the students. I feel it is necessary while you first are starting out to make sure you have some sort of income while you are building your clientele. I would say it takes about six to eight months to get a good base and a year to feel comfortable. Since my time was limited for education, I decided to go to Daniel Webster College and get a bachelor's degree in organizational management, aka business. This started me on the path of owning my own practice and doing a business plan based on my spa really got things started. I realized that I really wanted a larger space to start a day spa/clinic that had quality massage and outcall service that was not available in my area. In 2006 I got the opportunity to take over a 1,300 sq ft space in an athletic club and renovate it while still renting the small space I started in. With the help of my parents as silent partners, I proceeded with the build-out of my space and the hiring of my first sub-contractor. I started with one massage room and slowly built up to three massage rooms (one can be used for couples treatments), one skin therapist room, office, waiting room, restroom and storage/break room. I now have four massage therapists, including myself, and two skin therapists. I also keep a list of therapists I call on when I have large spa parties that come in.

The quote at the top is a big part of my life. Everything that has happened in my life has happened because of what I am focusing on at that time. An example of this is that my business plan (that was constantly happening in my head without me realizing or thinking about it) was house, good car, business, and family. In that order I received each item. Purchased my house in October 2005, renovated and opened spa March 2006, purchased a new car and was pregnant in May 2006, and had my first child December 2006! Crazy, right? Well, I didn't think about all of it until someone asked me how I got started and how I was able to handle everything in the recession. I did it because I had to. Failure wasn't in my vocabulary.

When I tell the story of how, what, when, it baffles me that I was able to keep it together but I just had that focus/perseverance, if you want to call it that. I just knew what I needed to do and having a child the first and third year in business definitely put a wrench in my workaholic lifestyle that a new business owner should have - or should they? Having a business and then instantly getting pregnant might not have been the best business plan but in hindsight it made me a better business owner. I had to work harder and smarter. I couldn't waste time because I didn't have it, so the first year I busted my butt. I still traveled the one hour and 30 minutes once a week to the city to work on outcall clients so I could pay myself and not take from the business. Once I got closer to having my son, I had to discontinue that and money got tight. What would I do without working? What would I do on maternity leave that I wasn't getting paid to stay home for? Luckily, the first therapist I hired as a sub-contractor to work with me was fantastic - brilliant even - and I didn't have to worry too much but when I had to have a C-section and my child was preemie, I decided to take three months off. I couldn't leave my baby and now I had two babies - my business and my son. Too hard to choose who gets the most of me, so I have to do for both. Letting go of the control was the best thing I could do. The more I trust and allow others that work with me, the busier I am. When I say busy, I mean my business, not just me. I would like to clarify: when you speak to a business owner and they say I/we are so busy, I always wonder if they mean them or their business. We, as business owners, will always be busy, so don't fool yourself and keep saying how busy you are, because in reality if you don't pay attention to that, you could go under in an instant! Whatever I attract in my life is exactly what I need at that time. The more you focus on not having money instead of doing something about it, the more time you waste and the more money you don't have.

I named this chapter "Letting go of the control" for one major reason. You can make good money doing massage but if you don't want to have to do all the work yourself for the duration of your massage career, you have to hire those that will help you. Hence letting go of the control. It's harder than it sounds. You are probably thinking: why wouldn't I want to do that? Think about it: no one does what you do. It may come close, but no one truly can do what you do in the massage treatment. But you have to trust in others' abilities to get over that control of your business. Now don't get me wrong, you will always need to keep a hand in your business - you are the face of that business, and the contact - but that doesn't mean you have to do all of the work. Learn to delegate. This will allow you to enjoy what you do and not stress about it. I still have trouble delegating but have gotten better over the years because I realized my strengths and weaknesses. I have always had my business phone as a cell phone so I could have it with me at all times. I didn't want to miss anything and this really helped me be involved at all times but, let's face it, you need a break or you may get overworked and resentful of what you are passionate about in your life.

Client contact is very important. There is nothing that says you shouldn't keep in touch with your clients. Technology today allows me to email, text and call any one of my clients and by doing this I keep in touch with them and see them more often.

An online marketing company is a fantastic tool and it's cheap to email hundreds of clients. That is a great reminder for your clients to think about you. You can send as many emails a month as you want, but I only recommend sending one or two. You don't want to give your clients too many emails or they get annoyed and then they will unsubscribe and you will have lost them. Your clients can unsubscribe if they don't want to receive any emails, but I try to focus on what a customer would want, such as specials and new treatments.

A monthly birthday special is a postcard that I mail out for the customers that sign up for my mailing list. This costs a little more but I feel it is a bit more personalized than an email. We give

20% off any one hour or longer treatment for the whole month of their birthday.

Products are another great way that I have boosted my sales in this economy. We sell facial products and that is what we use in all of our facial treatments. We sell products for after waxing, and gels and balms for massage injury clients. Every one of these items we use in our treatments - clients ask for what will help them and this is another way that we can help them and make more money.

We use a reception company as an answering service and it has an online system to book our appointments. It provides reminders via email or text to clients' cell phones, which cuts down on our cancellations and no shows. This costs an average of $100-$400 per month, depending on how much we forward the phone. This means I don't have to pay a permanent receptionist a salary but I don't miss any appointments/phone calls. Once appointments are booked, the therapists that are sub-contracted to me are contacted so many hours in advance of their appointments, when they are the same day, via phone. All other bookings are sent via email.

The best advice I can give is listen to your clients and take care of your body. If they ask to start face-down, do it. If they ask to have the room warmer, do it. Just do what they ask for and make sure you are not doing for your own interest/ease. This is not what they are here for. I stopped my sequence as soon as I realized it's not about me. You need to work out a couple times a week, visit a chiropractor, work with a trainer, get massage work done. What are we really doing all of this for? Really ask yourself this question and make a thought-out plan of what you do and do not want in this profession. My thought is: do what you love and the money will follow.

SHAUNA FLAGG BIO

Shauna Flagg lives in Wells, ME with her husband Greg, and sons Matthew and Jackson and black lab Shadow.

Shauna holds an Associates in Liberal Arts from New Hampshire Technical Institute and a Bachelors in Organizational Management from Daniel Webster College.

Shauna K. Flagg

Owner/Massage Therapist

Escape & Rejuvenate Therapeutic Massage and Spa

www.EandRMassage.com

C/o Seacoast Sports Club

Portsmouth, NH 03801

(603) 496-8802

Personal Info

(603) 491-9952 Cell

shauna1688@yahoo.com

"Fall seven times, stand up eight."

- Japanese Proverb

7

DON DILLON

If you think education is expensive....

My first practice was in a well-established chiropractic clinic. When my application was accepted as a massage therapist in this bright, modern and streamlined facility, I thought I had died and gone to heaven. The clinic enjoyed high traffic with two chiropractors, several chiropractic assistants, and me as the massage therapist.

For the opportunity to practice in this clinic, I agreed to pay 55% of my earnings. After some time, and a few conversations with colleagues, I became resentful of the contract because I thought that I was paying too much. I left the clinic to venture out on my own.

I soon discovered that, in fact, I wasn't paying enough to the chiropractor. My lack of skills and experience in operating a business quickly caught up with me, and I spent the next several years struggling to build a business. My rent was high to the chiropractic office because I was paying for the business skills and the traffic I did not have.

As Derek Bok said: "If you think education is expensive... try ignorance."

Working at another chiropractor's office, I finally recognized that I did not know how to build a practice. Inevitably this chiropractor severed our agreement because our percentage agreement was not generating sufficient return on his investment. And he had a more business-savvy therapist in the wings who would prove more profitable for him.

I was without a place to work, had minimal business skills and my wife was pregnant with our first child, which would mean three mouths to feed on one income. At a desperate time I was handed a book by my mother on personal finance. From there I began to study many other business books - marketing and sales, accounting and finance, customer service and communications, business systems and technology ... I was motivated to change my circumstances.

And change them I did. My income rose from $11,000 my

first year in practice to $54,000 at eight years in practice after beginning my "business education". Last year I had my greatest earnings yet - $69,500. In those early years I dramatically increased my income, simply by increasing my business knowledge and applying that knowledge to build skills and experience.

I am grateful for my early trials, for I do not believe I would have dug so deeply for transformative change had I not been pushed into a corner. I love my creature comforts as much as the next person and often when change is necessary I – unfortunately – wait until push comes to shove. However, with the grace and wisdom that can accompany age and experience, I am more open to challenges and to shed my old skin in exchange for growth.

In fact, it's my early experiences that push me to write on practice management issues and the opportunities and threats to our industry. As my impetus to keep writing and teaching, I retain in my mind conversations with many massage practitioners, often women and sole practitioners, who are hard-pressed to make ends meet. I believe my efforts will benefit them, and help position bodywork as a social ethos ... something everyone in society can access and benefit from. In a society riddled with violence, anguish and feelings of overwhelm, isn't bodywork one plausible answer to the suffering?

Meagan has asked me to pass on some wisdom "from the trenches" to budding massage practitioners but also for those seasoned workers who are still trying to make a go of things but are not earning enough to meet their needs. When I was in said position, this is what I wish someone would have shared with me:

Grow Service Capacity and Profits while You Moderate Strain.

The standard one-hour massage model is time and labor-intensive - fine if you're billing appropriately. However, many practitioners adopt the one-hour model of the spas but cut their fees almost in half because "my patients/clients won't be able to afford my rates". By squeezing my profit margin in a career that is limited by my body's endurance, I set myself up for poverty and eventually a forced vocational exit.

I would encourage the training of massage practitioners, whether spa or rehab focus, to adopt the use of methods (techniques) and modalities to both grow available service capacity - see more patients/clients in a day - while decreasing physical strain. Apply methods and modalities that boost your ability to deliver care while minimizing your physical wear-and-tear. More care, less wear-and-tear ... good mantra to follow.

In the spa industry, use body wraps, hot stones, various lymphatic massage devices to reduce direct hands-on application while still providing a solid spa experience. In the rehab environment, incorporate remedial exercise, contract-relax and other leverage methods, hydro and electro therapies, perhaps acupuncture to reduce your strain while delivering results.

You might argue "they expect one hour of hands-on time". They expect what you set them up to expect. I interviewed a practitioner for *Massage Therapy Canada* magazine who utilizes technology to film runners pre-and post-training, and assistants to move extremities during his soft-tissue manipulation. He billed $70 for a 15-minute session and grossed $150,000 a year. He was criticized by other practitioners, stating he wasn't providing real care. Did his patients come back? Did he understand their needs?

Did he get the results they were looking for? Oh yes, and he got results other practitioners could not, even with longer therapy sessions. Set expectations, educate your patients effectively on the process and deliver results ... you will be paid handsomely.

Educate. Educate. Educate.

When I graduated I thought I had a license to earn. "Now I'm a registered massage therapist," I exclaimed, "and people will beat a path to my door!" They didn't. "Massage" has many meanings to the public - some complementary and some not. Massage therapists don't enjoy the certainty gatekeeper health care providers funded by government Medicare programs do that they will be busy from the get-go. We must maintain professional skill and knowledge, uphold high ethical standards, but we must also continually sell, sell, sell the benefits of our work. For it is through continually putting ourselves out there, doing good work and educating the public, the media, the government, the insurance industry and the other healthcare providers that we will eventually change the current set of perceptions to more favorable ones.

In every visit - especially the first visit - I articulate the cause of the patient's condition, the effects (how the cause has played out in symptoms) and what remedy I'm planning to apply and deal with the problem. People want their problems dealt with, and if you can solidify your expertise and your good intentions in their mind, you will win audience to prove your intervention's efficacy.

Always get results on the first visit - use your intake and assessment to zone in on their primary complaint, measure it with range of motion, muscle testing, pain scale and other measures, and then retest post-treatment to show results have occurred. Having gained that person's confidence, you will never need to ask them to come back ... they will ask you for their next appointment.

Deliver your information in chewable chunks, from your business card, signage and website where they first become aware of you, to your intake, assessment and follow-up process, to regular informative newsletters (no. 1 practice retention tool!) and other direct mail pieces, even social media. Build a relationship over time, focus on educating, not soliciting, and you will earn the most coveted prize of all - their trust and respect.

Don't Discount. Stack the Value.

Social media sites can provide the inside story on what people of your interest are thinking. In my case, I dropped in on a conversation at one of the larger, popular social media sites for massage practitioners. The topic was discounting, and how much to discount. The tone of conversation seemed to suggest that discounting was common practice, and in fact expected. I asked: "Why set fees only to discount?"

From this and other posts I've read, it seems massage practitioners set fees only to counter them because "well, my clients/patients can't afford that". I think there's a deeper belief playing out here, and the practitioner's current situation (they're not making enough money to cover their expenses) is in conflict with other beliefs - "money is dirty", "I'm a healer, I don't do this for the money", or "I don't need much money to live". Incongruity between our circumstances and our deep-seated programming causes conflict, and to save the mind from going mad we rationalize. Then we compromise.

Meagan described the flak she received in writing her first

book *How to Make $100,000 per year as a Massage Therapist* from critics accusing that her intentions are entirely focused on money. I say to those critics: get some counseling. You're not helping yourself or anyone with these beliefs. Money can and is used for enormous amounts of good, and tens of thousands of massage therapists leave the profession every year because they can't earn a living from their work. Commit to earn a good wage AND do good.

So, don't discount. Instead, stack the value. Provide a thorough intake and assessment, get results on their primary complaint your first and every session, provide them with a bag of Epsom salts post-treatment, follow up with a phone call next day, send bits of information via a newsletter that is helpful to them, maintain a solid referral base of other practitioners helpful in restoring your patient's/client's wellness, constantly invest in your professional development, be available and get them in as quickly as you can, treat them as if they were your only patient/client ... if you stack the value, your fees can be considerably higher (and mine are) than other practitioners and these patients/clients will still come back to you. Trust, respect and value.

In special circumstances, when a patient has genuinely expressed an inability to afford care, I bill them at half my rate - but only in those cases and only for a set period of time. I no longer project my poverty mindset on them and imagine "they can't afford my fees".

Study the Micro and the Macro.

Again, the advent of the internet and associated technology has given us a tremendous opportunity to see inside the convictions and belief systems of others. Much advice on improving a massage practice success I've read comes up short. It focuses on the micro. That is, it focuses on what the practitioner can directly control – the product, the price, the promotion and the place (distribution) of that product. "Get a website" or "join a networking group" is helpful, but short of the mark.

Practitioners must also be aware of and comprehend the external factors – the macro –that directly impact our ability to practice. These come in the form of government legislation and taxation, relations with the insurance industry and other healthcare providers, our profession's culture, and public and media perceptions ... all interwoven into the broader socio-cultural context. Putting a website up will do you little good if you don't also monitor and respond to these larger macro issues.

Here is a list I've compiled and have reported on over the years:

Extrinsic Threats to the Massage Therapy Industry (RMT – Registered Massage Therapist)

- Workplace benefits claw back - disappearance of manufacturing and related jobs in North America and the recessive US and Canadian economies negatively impact employee benefit plans and worker utilization of massage therapy.

- Disproportionate taxation - in some provinces the Canadian government combined goods and services with retail sales tax, imposing greater taxation on massage therapy services from 5% to 13%. Competing services such as chiropractic and physiotherapy are not subject to these taxes. My concern: Registered Massage Therapists will absorb the tax within their profit margin for fear of business erosion, and squeeze themselves out of business.

• Massage as assistive care - auto insurance and workers' compensation requires gatekeepers to authorize Registered Massage Therapists access to funding = limits RMTs to providing care as secondary/ancillary health providers with limited access to capped funding.

• Growing competition - PT/OT assistants, kinesiologists and other support-providers to primary gatekeepers may provide massage and usurp Registered Massage Therapist employment. Profit motive of gatekeepers may dissuade referring down the street to RMTs and keeping profits in-house with hired assistants.

• Incredulous - insurers and governments are skeptical of Registered Massage Therapist results without degree-level education and evidence-based practices, and incredulity affects credibility and funding.

• Exploitation - lacking degree-level education, evidence-based practices and sufficient advocacy with funders leaves massage therapy profession vulnerable to commoditization by ignoble spas and massage franchises and restricted funding by government and the insurance industry.

- Change in workplace model - spas and franchises converting self-employed to employed RMTs. Practice management provided in exchange for autonomy, and sole-proprietors and small clinics will find it difficult to compete with high commercial exposure, large marketing campaigns, seven-day service availability and lower pricing.

- Threat to primary funding source - insurance fraud, associations with prostitution/illegitimate care are increasing, ongoing concerns to profession credibility

Intrinsic Threats

- Incongruent goals - massage practitioners lag behind other health disciplines in evidence-based practices, degree-level education, public relations strategy, school accreditation and regulation - thus credibility. Yet some practitioners oppose degree-level program and research as onerous and expensive - especially if Registered Massage Therapist is part-time/non-primary income

- Distrust of organizations - some Registered Massage Therapists oppose regulation and view regulatory process as cash-grab and intrusive, unsure of benefits of self-regulation or strong professional association

- Varying standards – Registered Massage Therapist teaching institutions display wide variance in quality of education and training. Non-accredited.

- Identity/brand confusion - spa therapist or rehabilitation therapist? Healthcare profession or personal service? All-inclusive tolerance by profession for broad scope of practice leads to marketplace confusion = lowered credibility, referrals and funding.

- Incongruent beliefs – Registered Massage Therapists vie for status and recognition; feel entitled to same bestowed privileges as other healthcare providers (without attaining degree-level education and evidence-based practices other professions have **striven for**). Believe massage therapy should be restricted from laypeople applying yet unwilling to pursue regulation and research demonstrating need for sufficient skill-set and therefore restricted application (controlled acts) to lay persons.

• Disorganization - professional associations struggle to convey value of membership/gain majority of Registered Massage Therapists as members. Insufficient membership reduces resources for advocacy and public relations.

Business management and success is more than operating the boat (micro) … you have to watch what the sea and the sky are doing and be prepared to respond (macro).

When Not Providing Care, Practice the Four "R's".

Of course providing care is your primary task in practice. But what if you've got an open appointment or two? Don't do the laundry, go shopping or sit on Facebook for an hour – unless these things will move you towards filling your appointment book. Yes, you will require some time each day for administration and operations, but keep it tight and focused. I recommend using those open appointment times to recruit new patients/clients, retain existing ones, reward referral sources and re-serve existing patients/clients by serving other needs they have.

Recruit – These are your ongoing promotional efforts to get your main message to your target market. Your campaign should include business cards, signage, brochures, website, direct or indirect mailers, advertising, public relations, information seminars, give-aways and networking. "But word of mouth is the best advertising...." Sure, if you have mouths wording positive endorsements for you. But if your practice is budding or floundering, don't wait for word of mouth. Recruit consistently and intelligently.

Retain – One US government study stated it takes five times the amount of resources (time/energy/money/people) to get new business than to keep existing business. General Motors found if they could keep you happy, your purchases with them could add up to $400,000 over your lifetime. It pays to retain existing business rather than always just chasing new business.

There are many ways to add value and increase your retention. Here are a few:

- Help people feel safe, warm and comfortable
- Confirm appointments
- Follow up next day after the first session to gauge response
- Provide Epsom salts/goodie bag on first visit
- Teach home care/remedial exercise
- Send a newsletter with essential tips and resources
- Recognize important dates (birthdays, anniversary of care)
- Ensure comprehensive care with an excellent team referral network
- Offer open appointments to non-recent clients/patients
- Reward referrals, loyal and frequent users
- Cultivate your skills & knowledge – be an SME (subject matter expert)
- Give back to the community

Reward – Do you treat all of your customers equally?

Although you should treat every one with professionalism, respect and good work, some customers are more valuable than others. According to Pareto's Law, 80% of your business comes from 20% of your contacts/customers. Some customers are more valuable than others - ensure they feel special.

Use your database to categorize referral sources (A), frequent users (B), and infrequent users (C). Keep a category (Q) for those you've become out of touch with over the last two years (don't erase … they may be back). Your job is to turn Cs into Bs, Bs into As, and keep As happy so they refer more people! Reward referrals with a small token gift or extra service time. Remember Pareto's Law.

Re-Serve – Many of the people you provide care for have multiple needs, and could benefit from some type of intervention between office visits. There are plenty of products and services both on the rehab and the spa side that your patients/clients can benefit from.

Use your monthly newsletter to promote a different condition … that's 12 conditions you're educating your contact base on a year. Chances are with each condition represented, your patient experiences that problem or knows someone who will benefit from your interventions. Find ways to serve your existing people more.

Isolation is the Enemy.

Earlier I discounted the premise of discounts. I suspect many massage practitioners make compromises like whether or not to offer a discount in isolation. Once we've left our training program we typically work one-on-one with clients or patients and interaction with colleagues is minimal. We don't have natural facility to check our assumptions, debate critical issues or question conventions handed to us. These conventions are no doubt well-meaning but are perhaps antiquated or inaccurate.

In an era of chat lines and email, social media, local and national conferences, trade publications and books like the one you hold in your hand, there's no reason to go it alone. In isolation, your judgment and business decisions lack the contribution of others, and you may be settling for compromises instead of real solutions.

Know Your M.O.

"Modus operandi" is defined as a method; a protocol; a

way of doing something. Your modus operandi (MO) determines how you deliver care - your location, pricing, products and services offered and how you promote your business. It defines the phraseology and methodology you use. For example, a spa therapist may wear a smock or spa uniform to provide "personal service" to "clients", providing longer sessions with a focus of "relaxation and rejuvenation" or "relief of tension and stress". The spa therapist may utilize hot stone, body wraps, essential oils and other spa applications to achieve results. Fees for services are typically higher than rehab settings and spas usually work with people who have manageable, non-complicated symptoms or are looking to experience wellness.

Contrast this with a massage therapist working in a rehabilitative setting, perhaps in the office of a physician, physiotherapist or chiropractor with "patients". The therapist wears medically-appropriate attire as do the other health care practitioners, and is savvy with completing auto insurance and workers' compensation claims. The treatment format may be shorter to fit insurance funding grids, include modalities such as TENS (muscle-stim/IFC) or ultrasound, and utilize remedial exercise with a focus of "treating pain" or a "myofascial dysfunction".

Why is it so important to establish your MO early on? From my conversations with members of the public trying to define massage therapy, the marketplace appears to be confused. "Massage" can mean many things – pain-relief (or, regrettably, pain causing!), relaxation, nurturing, rehabilitation, corporate wellness, personal care ... and of course many less favourable associations we'd rather leave behind.

It's our job to clearly define our service benefits in the minds of our target market. We never want to be ambiguous about our message, precluding our clients/patients from contacting or connecting with us. "I've experienced a workplace injury – does my massage therapist treat that?" Or, "I really need to relax and ease my stress ... where should I go for care?" Operating from a clearly defined MO will clarify your purpose and intention to the marketplace, making it easy for clients or patients to procure your services without confusion.

Your MO is very important to the financial stability of your business. If you take the spa model of one hour to deliver service, with the spa rate at $120 and you apply the same time and labour intensive service at $65-70 to a clinic setting, you may soon find your business bankrupt. The spa model serves a particular clientele offering personal services at a high premium, where the rehabilitative model works in the insurance realm with fee caps and limited coverage ... you can't integrate the two effectively. Again, your market determines your pricing, your product/service, your delivery method and your promotional strategy.

"I don't want to turn business away ... can't I offer both spa and rehabilitative?" I wouldn't recommend it, and I believe this is a main reason massage therapists have trouble sustaining a business. They diffuse the effectiveness of their promotion and application. Distil, don't diffuse.

There are at least four typical models of business operation - or modus operandi - in the massage industry: rehabilitative/clinical, spa, integrated/multi-disciplinary, and corporate wellness. In any of these models, massage therapists may be business owners, contractors or employees.

If your business is bleeding – having trouble attracting and retaining customers – perhaps your MO is not clearly defined and applied. Refuse to be all-inclusive and focus your business efforts and promotional campaign to clearly serve the needs of your target market.

In Closing...

Thank you for exploring with me a historical perspective of my growth and maturation as a massage therapist. I relish the opportunity to relive my struggles and triumphs. If just one massage practitioner reading this is able to extend and sustain their calling; to serve more people and heal more suffering; to be financially sound so they can focus on providing care ... then my contribution has been worthwhile.

I leave you with some words of wisdom from Socrates:

"Employ your time to improving yourself by other men's writings, so that you shall gain easily what others have laboured hard for."

DON DILLON BIO

Don Dillon, RMT is a therapist, national (Canada) speaker and author of two books. His articles have appeared in Massage Therapy Canada, Massage Therapy Today, Massage Magazine (online), and Massage Today (US). Dillon is cofounder of Massage Therapy Radio and can be reached at www.MTCoach.com

Don Dillon

relief@dondillon.ca

coach@mtcoach.com

19 Durham Drive

St. Catharines, ON   L2M 1C1 Canada

www.dondillon.ca

www.MTCoach.com

www.MassageTherapyRadio.com

(905) 937-5802

"Whatever you can do, or think you can, begin it. Boldness has genius, power and magic in it"

\- Goethe

8

MEAGAN HOLUB

"What is there left to say that you haven't already revealed in *The Magic Touch*?" a friend inquired when I told her I'd be writing this sequel. "Plenty," I replied.

I got lucky this time around. Rather than filling an entire book with my story and advice, I was offered the help of smart, savvy, one could say *superstar* massage therapists to share their journeys, struggles, and secrets. And while I could stop there and imagine that enough has been said, between the first book and the first seven chapters of this book, I won't. In business, even the business of massage therapy, things are changing quickly. The internet changes the landscape of business nearly every year. And yet, it is important for us to remember the basic standards of high quality service more than ever before. Though it has only been a short time since I began writing the first book, we have since experienced the toughest economic downturn many of us have ever witnessed. It affected our industry, as it did many others, in ways that required ingenuity and flexibility - and most of all it required us to take action. The interesting thing about a down-turned economy is that it forces you to take inventory of what is and isn't working in your business. And let's face it, in your life as well. The even more interesting thing about it is that if you remember the lessons you have learned in the slower economy, you will soar to incredible heights when the economic tide turns. So anything you find that works in the slower economy might just be your holy grail in the upturned ones.

In *The Magic Touch* I talked about putting my money into non-traditional places to build and support my business, discussed how I looked "outside of the box" and focused on economic factors I could control (my business), instead of ones I believed could entrap me in an uncertain and risky indebtedness (the housing bubble, for example). I warned of massage therapists becoming too heavily reliant on the luxury market and advised to seek out insurance clients as a way to keep consistent income coming in, no matter the state of the economy (accidents will always happen, we will always need health care). I presented ways to earn $100 per hour by branching into many different directions of this industry: travel massage, hotel massage, PIP and L&I, product sales. Even referring business to other massage therapists quickly builds to hit a high hourly rate, no matter the economy. What I knew then still applies now. Everything I believed when the economy was up, everything I preached to massage therapists who thought the "good economy gravy train" would never end - while I knew better - became even more valuable when the economy started down a slippery slope.

Here's the cool thing, from my perspective, about the uncertain economy. During a slow economy, every one of us is on level playing ground. None of us can say: "But they have more of x, y or z." None of us ever could, anyway, but I felt I'd make this point again. The truth is many of the massage therapists who sometimes felt they were working too hard in the "good years" slaving over insurance paperwork, while luxury massage therapists made amazing money and had the ultimate freedom, found their roles a bit reversed. All of a sudden the massage therapists who accepted insurance in their practices saw the best numbers they have ever seen, while those who were in a cash-only business model saw some of the lowest numbers in years. Life is truly a great equalizer. What goes up must come down. Where there is black there is white. You know how the sayings go. So rather than rehash what I said in the first book, I want to add value to your experience by telling you specific steps you can take in your business to increase your number of customers with a zero-dollar marketing budget in any economic climate AND share creative ways that you can capitalize in a downturn economy. Not because the economy will always be in a rut, but because if you can make MORE money in a downturn economy, you have done it based on efforts that are grounded in common sense, consumer satisfaction, and ingenuity - standards that will allow you and your business to flourish, whatever is thrown in your path. You have to strive to be the best in everything you do to thrive in a weak economy, and the reality is that this is the very same thing I said when I was describing how to bring in six figures in the first book. The message hasn't changed. Provide the highest quality service and provide value. Let people know what you are providing through effective marketing. The equation works only if you take action to create a business model that exemplifies these standards.

So let me share some ideas with you that are slow economy-focused with the intent of having you: 1) understand that every circumstance is profitable, and 2) step back and look at things from your clients' and referrals' point of view to see that it is so.

Let's first talk about your best source of referrals. These are the clients, professionals, friends and family to whom you are already connected. Do you have a way of communicating to them that you appreciate their business referrals and connections? It is becoming more and more common in small business to offer a referral fee or gift certificates to those who send business your way. Many massage therapists promote a "one free massage for every four massage referrals" program to their clients, which is a great place to start, but I think we can do even better. First of all, how do you market this benefit? Hopefully, you have advertisements in a visible area where the client checks in and out of your office, and you address this and other specials in your newsletter (which your client has had the opportunity to accept or decline when they fill out their initial paperwork). It's also necessary for you to ensure that everyone who comes in contact with your business understands you are one of the few savvy massage professionals who appreciates those who take care of you, so add this message to your business card. Coffee shops have punch cards, why can't we? I say we can and we should! Design a simple card with your business info and one small line underneath that says something like *"We believe in taking care to thank those who refer to us"* and have 4 or 5 holes at the top of the card with the word *FREE* under the last one. Talk about multitasking and being efficient… you have just let everyone - clients, potential future customers and referring professionals - know that you are a savvy business professional (which instills immediate trust), separated your card from the rest with its uniqueness, ensured that you never "forget" to tell a client about your offer, and encouraged skeptical consumers in with a "game" mindset. Everyone wants to win a prize. This only requires a few hole-punches to win. Everyone wins! And while you are at it, make sure the professionals in your life know that you appreciate their referrals and take the time to design letters for them to pass on to their customers with specials, coupons or deals designed especially for them. Educate professionals in your life as to: 1) how they can make their client relationships stronger and instill even more trust in their services, 2) which conveniences you bring to their lives, and 3) how you thank them for sending the best possible choice in massage therapy services (your company) to their clients.

This brings me to an important point. Contrary to what some believe, it is perfectly legal and ethical to provide cash referral fees to all business owners who send you clients, with the exception of medical providers, such as doctors and chiropractors, and some lawyers (laws are different in each state and country, so it is essential that you research your local laws and follow them to the letter). Some professionals such as hotel concierges simply will not send you business if you do not have a prearranged referral fee in place for them. Many more professionals, such as dance and fitness instructors, personal trainers, midwives, limo drivers, wedding planners and more, are expecting a small percentage as a "thank you" these days. I believe this to be a very cost-effective way to do business. If you get enough referring professionals sending clients to you, a marketing budget becomes totally unnecessary. The interesting part of this structure is that every dollar you spend on a referral will equal less than what you would have to spend on traditional marketing sources – and it saves you time. Traditional paper advertising can cost you thousands with no return. Saying thanks with 10% or 15% of the total cost of service, or with the gift of massage, whichever they prefer, is something you do AFTER you have already made money from the referral. Hence, you get to skip the ineffective, money-depleting tactics that typically don't work and cost a bundle. While some people get this confused with "giving kickbacks", I can tell you from extensive research and even talking with a CIA agent about this that we don't have anything to worry about if we work these arrangements out with those who aren't bound by "kickback" laws, such as injury lawyers, doctors, chiropractors, as mentioned before. But the true test of being ethical in this or any business arrangements is asking yourself this question: "Am I okay with my clients knowing about this arrangement?" If the answer is no, then you have some unresolved issue with the type of arrangement or the professional you are partnering with, and I believe you should not participate in it. For the rest of you, I suggest putting a disclosure on your website under "info" stating that you provide referral fees to anyone who refers business, so that everyone is on the up and up about your "affiliate program".

So now is a great time to explain to you what an affiliate is. If you look at the bottom of nearly every large company's homepage, you'll see a link to an affiliates program. Amazon.com is a great example of this. Basically, affiliates are companies with which you agree to refer their products or services and they agree to send you a pre-determined percentage of sales or a flat referral fee. Sound familiar? The truth is, nearly every blog that refers products has those products linked to an affiliate company. The blogger is likely being paid to tell you about that product. Here's the cool part: you can do this too. If you have a blog in which you are recommending products, or if you refer services and products to your friends on any social networking site, check to see if that company has an affiliate program. If they do, sign up and use it. You are already telling people about great stuff, so why not get a percentage for what you are already sharing with them? Let's take it a step further and talk about how you can receive referral fees. You have a service-oriented business, and when you get enough referring professionals sending you business, you will have clients requesting massages that you don't have time to schedule in, and services you are uninterested in providing. This is a perfect situation for you to refer business to other trusted massage therapists and keep a small percentage. These massage therapists will likely be grateful to give you a small percentage versus having to do the "businessy stuff" and/or work for peanuts at massage chains that seek only to take advantage.

There is a theme here that you might not see clearly, but I want you to. It's cooperation and sharing. I never understand why anyone would scoff at referral fees, and affiliate or partnership relationships when, from where I'm sitting, I see that these types of arrangements have made it so the little guys (us) can stick together and keep the wealth and resources between us. Why give thousands of dollars to a telephone directory that is owned by a billionaire somewhere, with no promised return on your investment, when you can give that money to someone in your small community? And when I say small community, that doesn't necessarily mean within a 10-mile radius of your town. I mean individuals who share common goals and motivations with you. The internet has created the opportunity to build what I refer to as a "global commune" for small businesses. We are able to share and refer resources and business with everyone who shares our ideals. It is truly an exciting time. I say, take the lessons from affiliate programs and the current big business bailout climate and learn from them. Apply the wealth-sharing to your dealings with local professionals and watch the amazing things that will happen for the growth of your company, and the development of yourself as a businessperson. It's time the little guys supported one another. Sharing is a second language to the professionals who contributed to this book. It can't be a coincidence that each of them is as successful as they are. Laura Allen has said her business is structured similarly in terms of compensation to the way mine was structured when I contracted 15 massage therapists, which is that we keep just enough of a percentage that we are provided for, the business can grow and maintain an excellent reputation, and the team is happy to come to work every day. Sharing with others gives you the opportunity to create things that you cannot create alone. So many people are afraid that if they refer business, they will lose that client. The irony is, if they can't see the new client, they will go somewhere else anyway and an opportunity to instill in their minds that you are customer service first, profit-motivated second, is lost. Whereas when you refer them elsewhere, they will often call you at a later date AND you will get a little thank you from your partnered massage professional. It's a win-win situation for everyone involved.

The current economy has awoken professionals to the fact that their hard-earned money should stay and be shared within their communities, but it has also created a spending environment more scaled back and conservative than previous years. Many massage therapists see this as a bad thing. I see this as a time of necessary change, and as a time of great opportunity for our entire profession to grow. Before you decide I'm totally bonkers, just hear me out. First of all, anyone who provides massage and accepts insurance is probably already nodding their head in agreement with this statement as they have likely seen their business GROW in the slow economy. Why, you ask? Because members are willing to take advantage of their insurance benefits more than ever before, that's why. If something is looked at as a benefit or value in this economy, it is more likely to be purchased, especially if that something is already partially paid for (insurance premiums). People have too much time on their hands and too little money in recession, so they want to take advantage of the luxuries available to them - "luxury" being a word still being used by consumers when they describe massage therapy. So whereas before, money was flying around and many clients didn't want to be burdened with insurance compensation, these days they don't have a choice.

Insurance billing can be very lucrative as your clients schedule up to tri-weekly per their doctor's prescription. If you accept insurances and learn the art of marketing towards the workers compensation and motor vehicle accident victims, you will have a predictable amount of income coming in, which has its definite benefits. As I said in *The Magic Touch,* for those of you who aren't averse to jumping through the insurance billing hurdles, it can prove well worth the effort. Use marketing headlines such as *"Been in a recent auto accident? Call today to find out if the other driver's auto insurance covers the cost of regular massage therapy"* or *"Hurt on the job? Call today to find out if you qualify to receive massage therapy through your Workers Comp coverage"*. You might be amazed at how many responses you'll get from people who never knew that massage was not only covered by insurance, but was also more than just a luxury service. And once they know the facts, they will tell all their friends who don't know either... and that is a very good thing for the growth of our industry, as well as our individual practices.

Recently candy and chocolate sales went through the roof. Know why? These things are small, affordable luxuries. If you look at all massage in the way that our customers do, it's easier to market to them. While many understand that massage is a valuable tool for maintaining health and vitality, when push comes to shove and times are hard, it's easy to see how massage might be budgeted out unless we offer them ways to continue getting appointments on their terms. Remember: they WANT to keep getting their massages. Thus far, I haven't seen many massage therapists take advantage of the opportunities to provide advantages for customers that would sway them in favor of continuing to get regular massage. In fact, I have seen a great number of massage therapists bellyache about the success of Massage Envy, but don't personally know of any who have learned from their model. It's not difficult to take the best parts of the Massage Envy model and work them into a concept that is both high quality and cost-effective. I am urging you to do just that. For example: recently there has been a resurrection of layaway programs in stores. Some online layaway companies allow consumers to make payments on even higher-quality products such as Apple computers and other high-end goods. By offering layaway to the consumer, they appeal not only to those who can't afford a large purchase all at once, and those who don't use, or can't obtain, a credit card. I wish I could say this is a brilliant new idea, but the reality is that this idea was around years ago. It's not new. We just find ourselves in a situation where stores benefit from the use of layaway again, whereas for years they wanted to benefit from the high interest rates of the in-store credit cards. They understand now:

either offer layaway or the product won't get purchased. Services these days are no different. If it isn't a necessity (in the customer's mind) and it has a large sticker price, I suggest you offer a layaway or payment plan. I also recommend that you "bold print" that you offer it on all your advertisements because it will make you the number one choice in massage businesses in downturn economies and give you a pretty good edge in upturn ones too. If you have questions about how to set up a layaway plan, I recommend you research the ones I mentioned previously and design one that similarly suits your business structure. This is also where accepting debit and credit cards comes in handy (I insist on accepting them in *The Magic Touch*) as you can get the client on a weekly, bi-monthly, or monthly auto pay program where you run the designated amount through on their selected dates and they get to budget in more massages than they previously thought they could afford. Payment plans are a great way to encourage regular client scheduling and provide them with a manageable way to pay for their beloved "luxury" massage. As if these benefits aren't enough, you also give the client a way to bond with a regular massage therapist (you) because of the payment plan, whereas before their only choice was to pay franchises monthly fees and hope that the massage therapist that they liked the month before hadn't moved on, as they tend to do.

So now you might be starting to see how perceived disadvantages in your massage business can actually be turned into advantages with the right "out of the box' mindset. Let's continue talking about this idea when it comes to "luxury" and "travel massage". Trying to bring a new market demographic into a luxury service in a slow economy is looked at as nearly impossible by most, but if you look what the service could be a substitute for, you begin to see a whole new picture. For example, answering the question "why are people buying more chocolate these days?" is an excellent starting point to answer similar comparative questions about our industry. Most likely the chocolate buyers really want a day at the spa, or a new handbag, or a brand new iPad. They feel deprived of what they really want and could get easily in a better economy... so they treat themselves to something smaller, easing the sense of deprivation. So now let's ask ourselves "what could massage be a substitute for that people are currently feeling deprived of?" The answer: so many high-cost luxuries I barely know where to start! So I'll start with the one that is most common - the yearly vacation. It is accepted by society that everyone deserves a vacation at least once a year. I don't know anyone who disputes this. We deserve to get away from it all once in awhile. A vacation a year is the least we can do for ourselves. So what happens when money is too tight to take the usual trip to Hawaii? I know what could happen... a couple's massage in a local hotel room or even in the home, depending on the budget. It is easy enough to market a "vacation at home" without mentioning money or budgeting. Marketing material such as: *"Why leave home for a vacation? Check into a local luxury hotel with your sweetie, buy a bottle of champagne and order up couple's massage with complimentary sugar foot scrub from us. You never knew vacationing at 'home' could be so relaxing."* will attract busy professionals, parents who can't get away any longer than a night, and couples on a budget quite effectively.

Likewise, I urge you to take a look at what locals in your area need and how their days are structured. If you are in a busy downtown area, perhaps you can offer an inexpensive lunchtime neck and scalp rub to busy professionals, or perhaps a foot massage after work is just the ticket for the ones who stand up all day. Or maybe you'll find the tech company across the way really needs your extreme carpal tunnel treatment a couple of times per week. Whatever it is, I bet it's right under your nose and you only have to price it fairly and market it in the right demographic. Everybody wants a little bit of luxury. Likewise, everyone knows they need to take care of themselves for their families as well as themselves. Find a way for them to easily and conveniently give to themselves, and I promise you they'll take it.

Whatever you take away from this book or *The Magic Touch* in the way of "thinking outside the box", ensuring you increase the number of clients that you bring in, or increasing your level of income... to do this you must take action. I know you've heard this before, but are you as effective at it as you would like to be? Taking action is a learned skill. Few of us were born action-takers and the ones who were probably had a lot of detention in grade school or likely were put on Ritalin as a kid. Modern life is not necessarily structured for the inventive, the go-getters, the creators, the enthusiasts and the entrepreneurs of the world... this is why they must design life to suit them. Every one of us is a person who can take action and achieve our goals. It takes baby steps to get to the top of the mountain. Just put one foot in front of the other. If you focus on each small task on the way to the whole, you will get there before you know it. If you stare at the top without motion for too long, you will likely psych yourself out. And a waste of a good dream is a damn shame.

Every Monday morning I type two weeks-worth of tasks out in a Word document titled "to do list" (I keep it simple around here). Then I go to work cutting and pasting the most important into the first five days of week one. Saturday is a "catch what I missed" day and Sunday is a day off. I leave the second week to be fine-tuned into separate days when I get to that following Monday, and so on. As I accomplish tasks, I delete them. Some get moved to other days. Some I do early. But here's the catch. Every task must be done in the week I allotted myself to do it, despite all other obstacles that come up. If not, I have to finish them that Saturday. Nothing motivates you like the idea of having to work on your day off to keep your promise to yourself. In fact, it is a Saturday as I write this. It didn't get finished during the week, but deadlines don't wait - not even ones I dictate for myself. Of course, I could move it to next week, but then what's the point? Why not move all my dreams, goals and actions to next week or the week after? Why even start? In fact, I could just move all my promises to myself to next week, and not stop there, but do the same with my promises to other people. But that is not who I choose to be in this life. Action is a choice. Keeping your word is choice. Reward comes with excellence, so at the very least give it your all. Everyone who contributed to this book gives it their all. Be inspired by them. Build your dream practice. Who knows, it might just be your story in the next book!

Laura Allen's goal was to bring in 365 new clients in a year. She hit that goal in early October. She had 74 more days to acquire new clients. Ann Ross, after being inspired by The Magic

Touch, decided to conquer her shyness and assume an educator role in the industry. She watched her business grow in leaps and bounds as an after-effect. What all the contributors to this book have in common, besides their profession, is the determined pursuit of their dreams. Call it stubborn, call it tenacious, I call it good business. I urge you to take any ideas offered to you by these good professionals and set goals for yourself. Create to-do lists at the beginning of each and every week and, come hell or high water, cross everything humanly possible off the list. Everything. As I said, if I am committed to excellence, to keeping my word, to achieving my goal... I have no other choice but to finish my list. I suggest you take what I am about to say to you to heart: you have only two choices: 1) take action towards your dreams, or 2) stay safe in your discontentment. I assure you, having been someone who has put all my energy into being on both sides of this fence, I will never go back to unhappy complacency. With all the challenges and fears that evolution brings, once you do it long enough, you can never return to a life that is less than you want to be. You achieve long enough, you realize it is only a matter of time before you can achieve anything you desire. All it takes is determination. The good news is that determination is a skill that anyone can learn. You don't have to be smarter, prettier or more talented to be determined. In fact, you don't have to be any of those things to be successful. You just need to take action in the face of all obstacles and fears. I don't just preach this, I know this. I am a living, breathing example of someone who beat all odds in my childhood, and knocked down the obstacles of poverty, serious illness, chronic pain and a destructive anti-money, anti-business mindset early on in my career (money and healing were oil and water - they don't mix, I naively told myself). I overcame a seven-year track record of low self-esteem and burn-out in the early years of my career as a massage therapist. And once I got momentum in being brave and taking risks and going where the demand and compensation was, not just where the other massage therapists were telling me to go, I began to realize that there were no limits in my career, or life. Now, I revel in the limitless. I went from $11,000 years to endless possibility. I am an author, mentor, corporation owner, and lucky to be mentored by some of the most-respected professionals in this business. My clients - celebrities, politicians and athletes, and "everyday" folks who are VIPs in my eyes - are the best clients I could ever ask for. I often say I am lucky, but when I honestly look back at my life, I know I created a lot of my luck by listening to the voice within, trusting it and following it with blind determination. There were times when my body was not healthy for me, times my mind was in fear, times all I could do was put one shaky, resistant foot in front of the other and close my ears to anyone telling me I was making a mistake. I still have to make the choice to block out a lot of influences. Negative media influences are a thing of the past in my world. People who seek to drain others in their interactions don't get any energy from me and are deleted from my life and business networking (I have deleted more than one social networking "friend", because with friends like these, who needs enemies?). I am unabashed about reaching my goals. I urge you to be the same. If you know yourself to be someone who is of good intent for the world and its inhabitants, shut out the naysayer and the bully. You don't need them. They are a dime a dozen. These types of people only deter your energy from getting where it needs to be to create meaningful things in this world. Creation is necessary now more than ever. Without it, we cannot evolve. And I believe we must.

So let nothing turn you back from your goal. Obstacles may arise, and that's okay - the path is rarely the way you imagined it. I haven't seen a straight and narrow one get you anywhere worth going, really. And it's the course changes that teach you the most valuable lessons. So don't get discouraged when things don't go according to plan. It might just be that your plan was shortsighted and the "universe" is helping you get there a better way. Be grateful and keep moving. This life is a gift. Never forget it.

MEAGAN HOLUB BIO

Meagan Holub is a Licensed Massage Therapist to the Stars, Author of The Magic Touch: How to Make $100,000 as... book series, is a WIBB blog contributor for Massage Today Magazine, and CEO of eMASSAGE, LLC. She has been featured in Massage & Bodywork Magazine.

Meagan spends free time mentoring Massage Therapists on Facebook, designing modern homes, traveling to exotic faraway places, and playing on the beach with her tiny beloved Pomeranian, Olive.

www.hundredthousanddolllarmassage.com

www.eMASSAGE.co

INDEX

A

B

business books, 188
business card, 52, 65, 67, 72, 122, 131, 134, 136, 137, 138, 193, 202, 218
business development, 111
business education, 189
business license, 84, 87
business skills, 188
business systems, 188
business-owner, 87

C

cancer metastasis, 22
cap out, 86
career, 9, 12, 15, 16, 17, 18, 21, 29, 59, 77, 78, 79, 86, 87, 88, 90, 96, 100, 101, 102, 104, 106, 121, 128, 148, 158, 166, 167, 172, 173, 180, 190, 235
Carole Osborn-Sheets, 158
carpal tunnel treatment, 231
celebrities, 235
chair massage, 9, 28, 29, 32, 33, 34, 35, 119, 172
challenges, 82, 83, 88, 105, 106, 107, 108, 158, 166, 189, 234
chiropractic clinic, 89, 96, 99, 187
chiropractors, 94, 119, 173, 187, 219
client attraction, 90
clientele, 89, 176, 208
clients, 10, 23, 26, 40, 41, 43, 45, 46, 47, 48, 50, 53, 72, 73, 89, 91, 92, 93, 98, 99, 100, 101, 104, 106, 107, 109, 118, 119, 127, 130, 134, 135, 136, 140, 141, 143, 144, 145, 147, 148, 150, 156, 157, 159, 162, 163, 165, 166, 173, 175, 176, 178, 181, 182, 183,190, 191, 194, 195, 202, 203, 204, 205, 206, 207, 214, 217, 219, 222, 225, 231, 233
clinical herbalist, 63
commercial exposure, 199
commission structure, 86
communications, 188
contract, 21, 48, 62, 69, 187, 191
contraindications, 123
corporate accounts, 81
corporate market, 32
cosmetology school, 79
cost-effective, 219, 227
cover letters, 122
Creative Loafing, 155
Cross-Referrals, 67

F

G

H

I

N

R

S

Other helpful, educational and inspiring books:

The Magic Touch: How to Make $100,000 per year
as a Massage Therapist – Meagan Holub

Better Business Agreements: A Guide for
Massage Therapists – Don Dillon

Charting Skills for Massage Therapists – Don Dillon

Masterpiece Massage: Maximizing Wellness
Between Sessions– Karla Linden

One Year to a Successful Massage Therapy Practice – Laura Allen

Plain & Simple Guide to Therapeutic Massage & Bodywork
Examinations – Laura Allen

A Massage Therapist's Guide to Pathology – Ruth Werner

Mosby's Fundamentals of Therapeutic Massage – Sandy Fritz

Business Mastery: A Guide for Creating a Fulfilling, Thriving
Business and Keeping it Successful – Cherie M. Sohnen-Moe

The Four Hour Work Week – Timothy Ferris

Linchpin: Are You Indispensable? – Seth Godin

Rich Dad Poor Dad – Robert Kiyosaki

The Seven Spiritual Laws of Success – Deepak Chopra

The 7 Habits of Highly Successful People – Steven R. Covey

The world of massage is constantly evolving.
Stay on top of innovations and be involved in discussion forums at
Meagan's Rubs to Riches Blog found at
www.hundredthousanddollarmassage.com

Join our community of MTs and others committed to the health
And well-being of every individual on the planet!

CPSIA information can be obtained
at www.ICGtesting.com
Printed in the USA
BVOW08s0920060417

480386BV00001B/98/P